Twayne's United States Authors Series

Sylvia E. Bowman, *Editor*

INDIANA UNIVERSITY

Elizabeth Bishop

ELIZABETH BISHOP

By ANNE STEVENSON

 105

Twayne Publishers, Inc.   ::   New York

To Mark Elvin

Preface

THIS STUDY of Elizabeth Bishop is analytical rather than descriptive or biographical. Apart from the first chapter, it does not concern itself with Miss Bishop's personal life; and as far as possible I have tried to avoid simply paraphrasing her stories and poems. The purposes of this book, then are: (1) to show how Elizabeth Bishop's poetry relates to the development of art in the twentieth century, especially to developments in painting and in literature; (2) to draw attention to the technical means by which Elizabeth Bishop has been able to give her poetry both particularity and universality; (3) to suggest that in many of her poems Miss Bishop reveals an intense concern with the relationship between nature and a moral interpretation of nature; (4) to show how Elizabeth Bishop's preoccupation with what I have called the ambiguity of appearances relates to discoveries in contemporary philosophy and science.

I have made no attempt to analyze all of her poems, for I believe that it is possible to "talk the very life out of poetry" as Miss Bishop herself has said. But I have tried, through suggesting possible ways of reading some of Miss Bishop's poems, to indicate the richness that is there.

ANNE STEVENSON

Cambridge, England, 1965

Acknowledgments

This book was completed and set a few months previous to the publication of Miss Bishop's new book, *Questions of Travel*, by Farrar, Straus and Giroux, Inc. in October, 1965. I am grateful to Messrs. Farrar, Straus and Giroux for permission to quote from "Manners," "The Armadillo," "First Death in Nova Scotia" and from the short story "In the Village." These are reprinted from *Questions of Travel* copyright © 1953, 1955, 1957, 1958, 1962, by Elizabeth Bishop. First published in *The New Yorker*.

I am exceedingly grateful to Houghton Mifflin Co. (Boston) for permission to reprint in full the following poems: "The Map," "The Imaginary Iceberg," "The Gentleman of Shalott," "The Man-Moth," "A Miracle for Breakfast," "The Unbeliever," "The Monument," "Cirque d'Hiver," "Jerónimo's House," "Little Exercise," "Cootchie," "Conversation" and "Rain Towards Morning." Other poems quoted in part from Miss Bishop's *Poems: North & South—A Cold Spring* are: "The Fish," "Roosters," "Faustina or Rock Roses," "At the Fishhouses," "Cape Breton," "A Cold Spring," "Songs for a Colored Singer," "Love Lies Sleeping," "Florida," "Invitation to Miss Marianne Moore," "The Prodigal," "Varick Street," "Chemin de Fer," "Sleeping Standing Up," "Insomnia," "The Bight," "Over 2000 Illustrations and a Complete Concordance," "The Colder the Air."

I am also grateful to *The New Yorker* magazine in which many of these poems first appeared. (Copyright © 1940, 1946, 1948, 1949, 1951, 1952, 1953, 1955, 1957, The New Yorker Magazine, Inc.)

Other poems first appeared in *Direction, The Forum, Harper's Bazaar, Life & Letters Today, The Nation, New Democracy, The New Republic, Partisan Review, Poetry, A Magazine of Verse, The Quarterly Review* and *Trial Balances*.

I should like to express my thanks to the Estate of Wallace Stevens and to Alfred A. Knopf, Inc., the publisher of the poetry of Wallace Stevens for permission to quote from the following copyrighted editions:

The Collected Poems of Wallace Stevens, Knopf, 1954.

Transport to Summer by Wallace Stevens, Knopf, 1947.

I am also indebted to Basil Blackwell (Oxford) for permission to quote from Ludwig Wittgenstein, *Philosophical Investigations* (1963); to Vassar College and the editors of the *Vassar Review* for permission to reprint some of Miss Bishop's early poems; to New Directions (Norfolk, Conn.) for permission to quote from the *Literary Essays of Ezra Pound* and for permission to reprint Pound's "In a Station in the Metro."

I wish to express my thanks to the librarians of the Watertown Public Library in Massachusetts who were so helpful in finding me material; to Brandt & Brandt of 101 Park Avenue, New York, who sent me many of Miss Bishop's unpublished poems; and most particularly to my husband, Mark Elvin, whose helpful suggestions and careful criticism made so much of this book possible.

Introduction

A WELL-KNOWN Harvard anthropologist once remarked that there are some ways in which a man is like all other men, some in which he is like some other men, and some in which he is like no other men. If the same can be said, in a limited sense, of poets, then this book has been written with a view to the ways Elizabeth Bishop is like no or few other poets.

The distinctiveness of most poets in the first half of this century was both interpretive and technical. That is to say, the aural sensitivity of T. S. Eliot and Ezra Pound, the visual particularity of Marianne Moore, the erudite colloquialism of W. H. Auden were, at the time Elizabeth Bishop was beginning to write, different stylistic expressions of the new and emerging sensibility which came to be identified with modern poetry. Far from being liberating, the demands early modern poetry made upon the abilities of the poet were very great. Pound and Eliot (who may be credited with founding the modern movement in so far as any movement in poetry can be founded) looked upon traditional forms as the roots of a decaying culture which they endeavored to resuscitate even while they deplored it. Their originality sprang from a self-conscious preoccupation *with* originality which existed in paradoxical conjunction with their reverence for the most rigorous disciplines of the past.

The first half of the twentieth century, therefore, was a time of anxiously controlled experimentation in which the ear, the eye, the imagination, the vocabulary, the linguistic sensitivity, the erudition—in short, the complete technical equipment of any poet—were subject to the most merciless scrutiny. After Pound, it was no longer possible to write "easy" poetry and survive in the literary world. All such nineteenth-century indulgences as derivative images and cliché metaphors, forced rhymes and trite emotions were energetically exorcised from the muses' temple—so energetically, indeed, that poetry has now come to have professional standards and to be taught in our colleges and universities as if it were an acquirable technical skill.

In the light of these developments, it is not surprising that a poet like Elizabeth Bishop, who is possessed of an ear and an eye which seem almost infallible and whose self-critical intelligence has restrained her from publishing all but a very little of her work, should in some measure be an eclectic poet. And I do not mean this statement in a derogatory sense. The respects in which *The Colder the Air* is a Metaphysical poem enhance rather than detract from its charms. There are rhythmical overtones of Eliot in these lines from "The Prodigal":

> Carrying a bucket along a slimy board,
> he felt the bats' uncertain staggering flight,
> his shuddering insights, beyond his control,
> touching him. But it took him a long time
> finally to make up his mind to go home.

and of Auden in the lyrical refrain of *Varick Street*—"And I shall sell you sell you/sell you of course, my dear, and you'll sell me."

Yet these respects in which Elizabeth Bishop is like other poets are accidental (she has never deliberately imitated anyone apart from some obvious pastiches) and technical. As a perceptive English critic once observed, she is one of those poets who has developed a distinctive *tone* without settling upon a particular *style*. There is some truth in this observation, except that one should add that tone, like style, is really a technical achievement; and to remark upon its excellence is to offer only a partial explanation of Miss Bishop's strength as a poet. Surely her principle strength is not technical at all, but consists of a profound instinctive awareness—a sense of what Japanese haiku poets called "the suchness of things"—which makes her insight meaningful in a context greater than that of a particular poetical fashion or period.

In this book I have tried to show how Elizabeth Bishop's poetry transcends its period—transcends even those excellences of form and image for which it has been most widely admired. The distinction I have tried to make is not one between form and content, for I do not believe that such a distinction can be meaningful except in a very superficial sense. I have tried to write, rather, of the undercurrents—the sources of resonance— of her poetry which form and content together seem to draw upon and at moments fleetingly reveal.

Most of Miss Bishop's poetry is very good poetry. Some of it is profound poetry. The suggestions this book offers as to why this is so are, of course, personal. I can only defend them on the grounds of my own feelings and from what I have been able to conclude in the course of a long and very helpful correspondence with Miss Bishop herself. She would be the first to deny, how- ever, that there are any absolute interpretations of her poems. With characteristic modesty, she remarks in a letter: "I believe that everyone has the right to interpret exactly as he sees fit." This book introduces Elizabeth Bishop in a way that I have seen fit. It is a presentation, not an explanation, of what she has written.

A. S.

Contents

Chronology

1911   Elizabeth Bishop born February 8 in Worcester, Massachusetts. Father was William Thomas Bishop, son of J. W. Bishop who had emigrated from Prince Edward Island, Canada. Mother was Gertrude Bulmer (Bishop) whose family lived in Nova Scotia. The poet's father died when she was eight months old and the child was brought up by her maternal grandparents in Great Village, Nova Scotia, and by an aunt in Boston.

1916   The poet's mother became permanently insane after several breakdowns. Her daughter never saw her again.

1927   Attended boarding school, Walnut Hill School in Natick, Massachusetts.

1930   First year at Vassar College in Poughkeepsie, New York.

1932   Summer walking tour of Newfoundland with a college classmate.

1934   Met Marianne Moore. Mother died. Graduated from Vassar with a Bachlor of Arts degree in English Literature.

1935-   Visited Belgium and France; spent the summer in
1938   Brittany, winter in Paris. Early in 1936 she went to England, North Africa, and Spain. Returned to the United States; spent part of the winter of 1936-37 on the West Coast of Florida. Traveled to Ireland, London, and back to Paris for six months in 1937-38, followed by some traveling in Provence and a short Italian trip.

1939   Moved to Key West, Florida. Loren MacIver, the painter, and her husband, the writer Lloyd Frankenberg, introduced her to John Dewey and his daughter Jane.

1943   Lived for nine months in Mexico. Acquaintance with Pablo Neruda, whose poetry influenced her.

1945-
1946   Received Houghton Mifflin Poetry Award for her first volume of poetry, *North & South*.

1946   Met Randall Jarrell who later introduced her to Robert Lowell. Friendship with Pauline Hemingway.

1947   Received a Guggenheim Fellowship. Spent a month at Yaddo in Saratoga Springs, New York.

1949-
1950   Consultant in poetry at the Library of Congress, Washington. Went to Yaddo again in the winter. Received American Academy of Arts & Letters Award.

1951   Awarded the first Lucy Martin Donnelly Fellowship from Bryn Mawr College. In November, started to travel around South America; visited friends in Brazil. Had a violent allergic reaction to cashew fruit and had to give up her trip to the Straits of Magellan. After she recovered, she decided to live permanently in Brazil.

1952   Received Shelly Memorial Award. Short stay in New York City.

1953   Two autobiographical short stories published in *The New Yorker* (June 27 and December 19).

1955   *Poems: North & South—A Cold Spring* published by Houghton Mifflin Company in Boston.

1956   Awarded the Pulitzer Prize for Poetry. Also a Partisan Review Fellowship for her book.

1957   Elizabeth Bishop's translation of the Brazilian classic, *Minha Vida de Menina* (*The Diary of 'Helena Morley'*) published by Farrar, Straus & Cudahy (New York).

1957   Awarded an Amy Lowell Traveling Fellowship.

1958   Returned temporarily to New York City.

1961   First traveled up the Amazon. Also made trips into the Brazilian "interior"—to Minas and into the Mato Grosso. Elizabeth Bishop, who has traveled extensively in Brazil since she went to live there, is presently working on a book of prose pieces about Brazilian life, architecture, music, and history.

1962   Awarded a Chapelbrook Fellowship. *Life World Library Series* published *Brazil* by Elizabeth Bishop and the editors of *Life*.

1964-   Since Miss Bishop moved to Brazil, she has been occupied
1965   with editing and translating Henrique Mindlin's new book on contemporary Brazilian architecture; has also translated prose and poetry from the Portuguese. Her third book of poems, *Questions of Travel,* appeared in October, 1965 (Farrar, Straus & Giroux). Houghton Mifflin has recently brought out a paperback edition of her first two books. Awarded the 1964 Fellowship of the Academy of American Poets; spent the summer of 1964 in Italy and England.

It is the glory and the misery of the artist's lot to transmit a message of which he does not possess the translation.

ANDRÉ LHOTE

All that we see could also be otherwise.
All that we can describe at all could also be otherwise.

LUDWIG WITTGENSTEIN

Elizabeth Bishop

CHAPTER 1

The Traveler

ELIZABETH BISHOP is an American in the fullest sense of the word. She was born in Worcester, Massachusetts (February 8, 1911); but both her parents were of Canadian descent, and her earliest memories are of the tiny village in Nova Scotia where she lived when she was a small child. Like so many American women writers, she went to Vassar College and later traveled abroad. Since 1952 she has made her home in South America, and it is with Brazil and the Brazilians that she has finally identifed herself—insofar as she has identified herself with any nation or people.

For Elizabeth Bishop's Americanism is as cosmopolitan as America itself. Her identity as a writer consists of a unique amalgam of qualities garnered from many sources and then subtly converted to suit the particular needs of her own personality. In one sense, her life may be regarded as a supreme intellectual, spiritual, and above all visual adventure, in the course of which she has formulated a way of looking and writing which is transcultural and transtemporal. At the same time, she has always been passionately committed to a set of esthetic values that has determined the scope of her vision. The range of her life has been measured by her sensibilities as an artist. Her work is characterized by a paradoxical combination of breadth and astringency, of freedom and restraint.

I

Elizabeth Bishop's family, on her father's side, was prosperous and middle class. Her father, Thomas Bishop, a builder, was the eldest son of the founder and director of J. W. Bishop &

Sons, at one time famous in the Boston area for its public buildings—the Boston Public Library and the Museum of Fine Arts among them.

John W. Bishop, the poet's grandfather, came from White Sands, Prince Edward Island, off Nova Scotia. He was the son of a Canadian farmer but, so the story goes, ran away from home at the age of twelve with a box of carpenter's tools on his back. He went first to Providence, Rhode Island; then, having made a "good marriage" (his wife was a Miss Sarah Foster of an old New England family), he settled in Worcester where, in due course, he made his fortune. His history is characteristically American and bears all the earmarks of the success story: early adversity, enterprise, perseverance, luck, love, and a happy ending. It is no surprise to learn that John Bishop was one of the first citizens of Worcester to own an automobile.

Thomas, his son, who grew up in well-to-do surroundings, was apparently well educated. He seems to have been a gentle, handsome, modest man with literary tastes and some sensitivity. Rather late in his life, when he was thirty-seven, he married a Canadian girl ten years younger than he, Gertrude Bulmer, poor and country bred in the beautiful Acadian countryside of Nova Scotia. The marriage, however, lasted only three years. Eight months after the birth of their daughter, Elizabeth, Thomas Bishop suddenly died. His wife never recovered from the shock. Whether her nervous collapse and subsequent insanity were entirely a result of her husband's death or whether her disease was an affliction of long standing is impossible to say. The tragedy remains. At the age of eight months Elizabeth Bishop lost, in effect, both parents. She was taken at once to live with her mother's family in Great Village, Nova Scotia, and it was there that she spent her early childhood.

The Bulmers were descended from a family of New York State Tories who had been given land grants in Nova Scotia at the time of the American Revolution. The family had settled in Great Village and in the course of time intermarried with its

predominantly Scottish and Irish inhabitants, although there
were always many ties with England. Grandfather Bulmer owned
and ran a local tannery until local tanning vanished; then he
farmed in a small way, as did almost everyone else in Great
Village. His wife was the daughter of a sea captain, William
Hutchinson, famous among the villagers for having been lost
at sea with all hands in a famous storm off Sable Island. Elizabeth Bishop may owe much to the Hutchinson side of her
family, for its members seem to have had the intelligence,
talent, adventurous spirit, and love of the sea which have
distinguished her own life. Three of her Hutchinson uncles
were Baptist missionaries in India; another, George Hutchinson
(of the poem *Large Bad Picture*), ran away to sea at the age of
fourteen and later settled in England where he became a painter.

Great Village itself lies in the rich farming country around
the head of the Bay of Fundy. Neat and well-preserved, it is
like a small New England village, with its white painted houses,
elm trees and large white church in the middle, designed, it is
said, by the painter, George Hutchinson. In this part of Nova
Scotia, with its dark red soil, blue fir trees, birches, and clear
rivers running into the bay, life was nearly as idyllic and backward as it had been for Longfellow's Evangeline. The Bulmers
made their own yeast and butter. There was no electricity, of
course, and no plumbing. Elizabeth attended the primer class
in the country school where the children were provided with
bottles of water and rags to wipe their slates. Like most of the
inhabitants of the village, the Bulmers were Baptists; and
Elizabeth's aunts, who were musical, sang in the choir. Grandfather Bulmer was a deacon. When he passed the collection
plate on Sunday, his granddaughter remembers, he used to
slip her a strong white peppermint with CANADA written across
it. This grandfather, sweet tempered, devout, and fond of
children, was always a favorite with her. The poem "Manners,"
published in 1955 in *The New Yorker*, recalls his kindness and

old-fashioned dignity which survived the incursions of the twentieth century.

> My grandfather said to me
> as we sat on the wagon seat,
> "Be sure to remember to always
> Speak to everyone you meet."
>
> We met a stranger on foot.
> My grandfather's whip tapped his hat.
> "Good day, sir. Good day. A fine day."
> And I said it and bowed where I sat.
>
> . . . .
>
> When automobiles went by,
> the dust hid the people's faces,
> but we shouted "Good day! Good day!
> Fine day" at the top of our voices.
>
> When we came to Hustler Hill,
> he said that the mare was tired,
> so we all got down and walked,
> as our good manners required.

After her husband's death in 1911, Gertrude Bulmer Bishop, under the care of her devoted sister, Grace, was taken to McLeans Sanitarium on the outskirts of Boston for treatment. Her condition did not improve there, however, and she returned in 1916 to her home and family in Nova Scotia in the hope that, in familiar surroundings, she might recover. But the visit ended in tragedy. Her final breakdown occurred that summer; and, since she had lost her American citizenship when her husband died (regulations regarding married aliens were more stringent then than now), she could not return to McLeans but had to go instead to a mental hospital in Dartmouth, Nova Scotia. In Massachusetts the Bishops did all they could to facilitate her return, sparing themselves neither effort nor expense, but without success. She remained in Canada, permanently insane; and, although she did not die until 1934, her daughter never saw her again.

II

Out of the horror and pathos of these events Elizabeth Bishop later made a short story. "In the Village"[1] describes, without sentimentality but with immense feeling, a child's experience of adult suffering. As the story opens, the terrible scream of the mother hangs indelibly in the blue Nova Scotian air, but mingled with it is the clang of the blacksmith's hammer, beautiful and pure. Between these two poles of sound the story is, as it were, suspended in the memory of the child; however it is not a child who tells it but an adult who remembers childhood in its perfect, illogical fragments. Time seems, therefore, not to be chronological but dramatic. Events have a symbolic quality, but they are at the same time meticulously realistic.

"In the Village" begins on a hot summer afternoon. The dressmaker is "crawling around and around on her knees eating pins as Nebuchadnezzar had crawled eating grass," fitting the mother for a new purple dress. But the mother is too thin. The dress is all wrong. There is a scream, and the child disappears. In the background, the sound of the blacksmith's hammer continues.

> Clang. Clang.
> It sounds like a bell buoy out at sea.
> It is the elements speaking; earth, air, fire, water.

Later the child visits the blacksmith's shop as the mother and the three sisters "sit on the back porch sipping sour, diluted ruby: raspberry vinegar." Nate, the blacksmith, wears a "black leather apron over his trousers and bare chest, sweating hard, a black leather cap on top of the dry, thick, black and grey curls, a black sooty face. . . . The horseshoes sail through the dark like bloody little moons to drown in the black water, hissing, protesting. . . . The attendant horse stamps his foot and nods his head as if agreeing to a peace treaty. Nod

> And nod."

In such details, accurate and resonant, the summer uneasily

passes; the child observes it with curious detachment as she takes the cow to pasture every day through the familiar village and passes the familiar houses, the church, the store. Then one night there is a fire in a neighbor's house. The grandmother and aunts are frantic. Soon afterwards the mother disappears; the front bedroom is empty. Parcels are sent each week containing fruit cake and chocolates. Life in the village goes on, but it is not the same, for the scream hangs above it: "Flick the lightning rod on top of the church steeple with your fingernail and you will hear it."

Yet, at the same time, on either side of the scream, there flows another sound, another element represented by the blacksmith, by the cow making cow-flops along the path, by the horse waiting patiently to be shod. Against the theme of personal tragedy runs a countertheme of apersonal existence. Human anguish is only part of a world which also contains animals, smells, and colors. In the mind of the child, the human and the other-than-human worlds coexist in a kind of harmony which, possibly, only a child can know.

The same theme appears again in another autobiographical story called "Gwendolyn."[2] This time it is the death of a little girl, a playmate of the author when she was a child, which is treated both as a traumatic revelation of mortality and as a simple, though frightening event, which is part of a sequence of other, quite normal occurrences: bronchitis, church picnics, and the arrival and departure of relatives. Gwendolyn's death is terrible. To the child watching through the lace curtain of the parlor windows, the sight of the little coffin, lying all alone on the grass by the church door, is so agonizing that she runs howling to the back door and out among the hens, with her grandmother weeping, after her. Yet the funeral takes place, the insupportable moment passes, and Gwendolyn becomes a pretty memory. Her image is perpetuated in the shape of a beautiful doll, named after her and brought out as a treat for special occasions.

III

Elizabeth Bishop seems to me rare among contemporary writers in that she has preserved, not only in these stories but in much else that she has written, this distinctively childlike vision with regard to human tragedy. This observation is not meant to indicate that she is naive; rather, I mean that for all her witty sophistication—and many of her poems are very witty indeed—she has refused to be theoretical about life. She has accepted what she has seen, and she has faithfully observed a great deal. But she has never developed her observations into a philosophy, never explicitly associated them with a central core of thought or belief.

For her poetry, this reluctance to theorize has been both an advantage and a disadvantage. It has been an advantage because it has liberated her from the necessity of explaining those aspects of life which she has been so supremely capable of expressing symbolically. The world in which she is most at home— that of vision and fantasy—is very different from the world of philosophy and analysis. It is dangerous and difficult, and perhaps not the task of the poet, to amalgamate the two. On the other hand, it is difficult for a poet to come to terms with life, with its moral and emotional problems, without some theoretical apparatus. What one often seeks in reading the whole of a poet's work is a sense of growth, of what might be called a development in understanding. The poetry of Yeats, for instance, shows such a growth. In another way, so does that of T. S. Eliot. But Elizabeth Bishop's work, elegant and eloquent as it often is, does not achieve this kind of organic unity. Whatever ideas emerge have not been arrived at over a period of time but perceived, it would seem, in passing. They are the by-products of her meticulous observations.

There is, however, one aspect in which her work may be said to be philosophical; and this, although it is nowhere explicitly stated, is important to understand if we are to appreciate the special quality of her perception. It has to do with her concept of nature; it is the very quality which gives such poignancy to the short stories "In the Village" and "Gwendolyn." And it may be expressed rather simply. Nature, for Elizabeth Bishop, never makes concessions to the aspirations and desires of human beings. It is the apersonal, amoral condition of life; it is the fact of existence which man, whatever his hopes, must reckon with as best he can.

In one sense this view places her in the mainstream of New England writers who, over a hundred years ago, felt so keenly the organic connection between man and nature. Plainly, she does not, like Emerson and the Transcendentalists, regard the outward aspect of nature as a veil of seeming or "divine dream from which we may presently awake to the glories and certainties of day."[3] But Miss Bishop is greatly in debt to Herman Melville and not a little to Nathaniel Hawthorne, whose novels attribute man's tragedy largely to his own sense of evil—to his will which strains against nature and to his mind which endows nature with moral power. Melville, in *Moby Dick* and even more strikingly in his last novel, *Pierre* (which significantly bears the second title of *The Ambiguities*), anticipates Elizabeth Bishop's quieter assumption that any real distinction between good and evil is man-made; that objectively, with regard to man's spiritual struggles, nature remains absolutely neutral.

Robert Lowell, another contemporary poet whose roots go back to seventeenth-century Massachusetts, is equally aware of the terrifying unhumanness of nature; but, like Hawthorne, whom he resembles in other ways too, Lowell is preoccupied with the moral nature of man, not with the amorality of the world, and his poetry is a study of guilt and madness. Elizabeth Bishop, although the reader feels she is aware of an interior anguish, is detached from it in her poetry. Man, for her, appears as a figure in a landscape, flawed, helpless, tragic, but capable also of love and even of happiness. Love and happiness are, however, contingent on a condition of naturalness: they depend upon man's capacity to live simply, in harmony with a natural environment, upon his lingering sense, fast disappearing in a world of technological "progress," of what the Chinese sage Lao-tzu is said to have called "Primal Unity." A simple, unworldly society such as that of Great Village could absorb human tragedy as the sound of the blacksmith's hammer absorbed the scream of the insane woman. Provincialism, far from being the breeding ground of guilt and suspicion that Hawthorne and Robert Lowell have envisaged, is, in Elizabeth Bishop's view, the last bastion of innocence.

This instinctive sympathy for simple, unsophisticated people has meant that when Elizabeth Bishop writes of people at all—and often she leaves them out of her landscapes—they tend to be childlike in their apprehension of life, if not actually children. The first book she translated into English from the Portuguese after she went to live in Brazil was, characteristically, the diary of a real little girl whose life in an isolated Brazilian mining town must in some ways have resembled her own early life in Nova Scotia.

The Diary of 'Helena Morley' (in Portuguese, *Minha Vida de Menina* or *My Life as a Young Girl*) is, in fact, a book which expresses Elizabeth Bishop's humanity and purity of spirit more explicitly than anything that she herself has written. When the diary was written at the turn of the century, its Anglo-Brazilian author was between the ages of twelve and fifteen. The diary was published in Portuguese in 1942 when the young "Helena" was grown. At that time Helena contributed an introduction to it, part of which is quoted here because it so clearly suggests Elizabeth Bishop's own moral attitude.

And now a word to my granddaughters: you who were born in comfortable circumstances and who feel sorry when you read these stories of my childhood, you do not need to pity poor little girls just because they are poor. We were so happy! Happiness does not consist in worldly goods but in a peaceful home, in family affection, in a simple life without ambition—things that fortune cannot bring and often takes away.[4]

Helena's world was indeed a happy one, although tiny and self-contained. It was full of incidents and crammed with personalities: parents, brothers, a sister (of whom Helena is inordinately jealous), a variety of aunts, uncles, and servants, and a devoted grandmother, who is really the alter-heroine of the narrative and whose death toward the end provides it with a degree of tragic stature. The book is a masterpiece not only because it is true—as Elizabeth Bishop points out in her introduction, one of its charms is that "it really happened"—but because it is entirely unselfconscious. The child it reveals is a natural child whose mind, at once joyous and sad, superstitious and rational, idealistic and practical, accepts the "suchness" of life with an equable sensitivity. Helena, with all her faults and virtues, her worries, her disappointments, and her triumphs, is a small archetype of life itself. She is a living testimony of both its richness and its evanescence.

Elizabeth Bishop must have been a child very like Helena during the years when she lived with her grandparents the Bulmers in Great Village. When she was taken, at six, to live with her paternal grandparents in Worcester, the peaceful home, the family affection, and the simple life she had known in Nova Scotia vanished. The change was like a fall from innocence and she never forgot it.

Part of her unhappiness in Worcester was simply due to ill health. She had suffered from severe bronchitis in Great Village before she went to Massachusetts, and in Worcester it became much worse. Acute asthma, eczema, and even symptoms of St. Vitus' dance developed; and the accumulation of diseases almost killed her. Her grandfather appealed to her mother's sister, the poet's Aunt Maud who was married but childless, and she took Elizabeth to live with her in Boston. Slowly the child's health improved, but she could never attend school regularly. Instead, she spent long, solitary winters in bed, reading. Her passion for books and for music dates from this period (she was about eight) when, sick and without friends of her own age, she began to write poems and to take piano lessons.

When she was thirteen, she was well enough to go to a summer camp at Wellfleet, on Cape Cod. There she learned to sail— a sport which she has been fond of all her life—and made a few friends. Later, when she was sixteen, she went to boarding school at the Walnut Hill School in Natick. But apart from summers, some spent in Great Village and six of them at Well-fleet, Elizabeth Bishop's childhood was lonely. Shy, chronically afflicted with asthma and bronchitis, and, in spite of the affectionate devotion of her aunts, without the irreplaceable love of a mother or father, she found, as so many solitary children have, a much more congenial and sympathetic world for herself in books.

At fifteen, she loved Whitman; at sixteen, she was given a volume of poems by Gerard Manley Hopkins and was so excited by it that she learned almost all the poems by heart. When she went to Walnut Hill, a sympathetic English teacher urged her to read Shakespeare and the English Romantic poets, lent her books, and encouraged her to write. But not until she went to Vassar College did Elizabeth Bishop begin to meet people whose intelligence and perception were equal to her own. The college at that time reflected generally that atmosphere of liberalism and experimentation which has come to be associated with the 1930's in America. Bohemianism, like radicalism, was very much "in the air"; Edna St. Vincent Millay had attended Vassar not long before and had left succeeding generations bobbing in the wake of her reputation; Mary McCarthy, author of *The Group,* was a year ahead of Elizabeth Bishop (who is not, however, represented in Miss McCarthy's novel) and was, as she still is, a close friend.

At one time Mary McCarthy, Elizabeth Bishop, and a few others started a rival "modern" literary magazine to protest against the policies of the established *Vassar Review*. Later they were invited to join the *Review*, and the two magazines amalgamated. But there was apparently always a conflict between the "intellectuals" and the more ordinary Vassar girls. In one issue the *Vassar Review* published a page of caricatures—rough sketches of Elizabeth Bishop and two of her friends—over the caption "The Higher Type." It is probable that her intelligence and shyness, together with a certain aloofness of manner, made her seem inaccessible to many of her contemporaries. But she had many close friends, and in her senior year was editor of the college yearbook as well as a regular contributor to the *Vassar Review*.

IV

The contributions Elizabeth Bishop made to the *Vassar Review* are exceptionally mature, but her poems are remarkable more for their technical proficiency than for the depth of feeling they reveal. At their best they are clever pastiches of sixteenth- and seventeenth-century Metaphysical verse:

> Love with his gilded bow and crystal arrows
>> Has slain us all,
> Has pierced the English sparrows
> Who languish for each other in the dust,
> While from their bosoms, puffed with hopeless lust
>> The red drops fall.

There is humor and cleverness in these lines but little warmth. The young Elizabeth Bishop was very guarded about her emotions; she preferred, in almost all cases, ice to fire.

Many of her early poems are macabre, dream-like poems which show the influence of writers like Rimbaud and Poe. One of these, entitled "Some Dreams They Forgot" anticipates another and much more finished poem, the last section of her "Songs For a Colored Singer" which appeared in *North & South* (1945). In both poems there is a mysterious metamorphosis as

black drops which fall out of a night sky turn into seeds. The
earlier poem is a sonnet, but its rhythm is freely broken up and
resembles Hopkins' "sprung rhythm" in that it maintains five
beats in each line but disregards the number of syllables between
them.

> The dead birds fell, but no one had seen them fly,
> Or guessed from where. They were black; their eyes were shut,
> And no one knew what kind of birds they were. But
> All held them and looked up through the new far-funneled sky.
> Also dark drops fell; night-collected on the eaves
> Or congregated on the ceilings over their beds,
> They hung, mysterious drop-shapes, all night over their heads
> Now rolling off their careless fingers quick as dew off leaves
> Where had they seen wood-berries perfect black as these,
> Shining just so in early morning? Dark-hearted decoys on
> Upper-bough or below leaf. Had they thought poison
> And left; or—remember—eaten them from the loaded trees?
> What flowers shrink to seeds like these, like Columbine?
> But their dreams are all inscrutable at eight or nine.

The tone of this poem—its questioning, its uncertainty, its
ambiguity, and its mysterious precision which seems to point
at something which is perhaps not there after all—is one that is
developed over and over again in later works. Here, for instance,
is the passage already mentioned from "Songs for a Colored
Singer":

> Then the dew begins to fall,
> roll down and fall.
> Maybe it's not tears at all.
> See it, see it roll and fall.
>
> Hear it falling on the ground,
> hear, all around.
> That is not a tearful sound,
> beating, beating on the ground.
>
> See it lying there like seeds,
> like black seeds.
> See it taking root like weeds,
> faster, faster than the weeds,

all the shining seeds take root,
conspiring root,
and what curious flower or fruit
will grow from that conspiring root?

Fruit or flower? It is a face.
Yes, a face.
In that dark and dreary place
each seed grows into a face.

Like an army in a dream
the faces seem,
darker, darker, like a dream.
They're too real to be a dream.

In this sing-song, rhyming "spiritual," Elizabeth Bishop manages to create the same impression she did in her early sonnet. Here is the same unearthly, eerie world she seems to apprehend by crossing the boundary between consciousness and subconsciousness with her eyes open. The uniqueness of her vision is that it extends into the regions of dream and fantasy without ever taking leave of the touchstone of the senses. Often the reader feels that she keeps her poems in strict forms *in order* to bring them into line with ordinary experiences: the poems themselves become bridges from one world into another. For this reason, although she has been much interested in Surrealism, she is not a Surrealist poet. Her "dream" poetry is a far more subtle achievement. She has described subconscious experience without trying either to explain it or to imitate it. Her poems are often haunting because they are neither didactic nor apocalyptic; they are simply descriptions which seem to be empirically true.

The poem "The Unbeliever" provides a good example of Elizabeth Bishop's genius in this respect:

He sleeps on the top of a mast
with his eyes fast closed.
The sails fall away below him
like the sheets of his bed,
leaving out in the air of the night the sleeper's head.

Asleep he was transported there,
asleep he curled
in a gilded ball on the   mast's top,
or climbed inside
a gilded bird, or blindly seated himself astride.

"I am founded on marble pillars,"
said a cloud. "I never move.
See the pillars there in the sea?"
Secure in introspection
he peers at the watry pillars of his reflection.

A gull had wings under his
and remarked that the air
was "like marble." He said: "Up here
I tower through the sky
for the marble wings on my tower-top fly."

But he sleeps on the top of his mast
with his eyes closed tight.
The gull inquired into his dream,
which was, "I must not fall.
The spangled sea below wants me to fall.
It is hard as diamonds; it wants to destroy us all."

"The Unbeliever" is an excellent example of how a purely
visual image in poetry can be more emotionally powerful than a
logically consistent metaphor. The question of what the unbeliever does not believe is never clarified. The picture alone
is everything, and it is in the picture, not in an abstract paraphrase of it, that subjective human emotions (irrational terror,
acrophobia, instinctive fear of engagement in life) find concrete expression. It is possible to suggest an interpretation of
this poem, but it is not possible to explain it. We may imagine,
for instance, that the unbeliever who sleeps on the top of a mast
with his eyes shut is a man who is afraid to believe in the fixity
and benevolence of the universe—and who may be right to be
afraid. His position *is* precarious; his dream is, as far as he
knows, a true one. The lies perpetrated by the gull and by the
cloud (both believers) only show that his fear is justified. For

both the gull and the cloud are believers whose belief, although false, is irrelevant to their survival. The cloud only imagines that it is founded on marble pillars; the gull only imagines that his wings and the air through which he travels are made of marble. Belief, then, is shown to be only an attractive deception; and the achievement of the man is that he manages *not* to believe. Yet he is not a realist either, for he knows only what he dreams. He knows only how not to believe what the gull and the cloud tell him.

Even with such an interpretation in mind, the poem is extraordinarily evasive. Why, for instance, does the man keep his eyes shut? This condition suggests that the believers have their eyes open: that, in fact, it is only those who believe who are able to participate in "real" life. Paradoxically, unbelief seems to cripple action, to force the unbeliever into a false position (the gilded ball). This, perhaps, is why "The Unbeliever" is at once so intriguing and so unsatisfactory a poem. Absolute agnosticism —and certainly this is what, intentionally or not, Elizabeth Bishop is expressing here—is a theme which may have to seem unsatisfactory; that is, agnosticism means that we can never know anything absolutely. There is an element of doubt in the commonest occurrences of life. A man, whatever his pretensions to freedom and wisdom, is always a prisoner of his own mind. And these are themes which recur again and again in Elizabeth Bishop's poetry and are, in the end, sources of its resonance (see Chapters II and V).

V

While Elizabeth Bishop was at Vassar, she wrote a number of short stories which are so trenchantly witty and perceptive that it would be a pity not to mention some of them. In one, "Pope's Garden," Nature visits Alexander Pope's garden at Twickenham. (The story was apparently written for an English class.) She learns that Pope has built his grotto especially in honor of her, and at first she is delighted: "All this for me!" she cries. The author "sends for cocoa and orange cakes powdered over with sugared violets" and offers to show Nature around. Yet something is wrong. Nature's sensibilities do not seem to be in sympathy with Pope's. As she observes the painted grottos and the artificial waterfalls, she becomes visibly annoyed. "Paint! Design!" she exclaims at the end, "Heaven forbid!" And Nature retreats in a huff as Pope's carriage rounds the bend of his drive.

In another story, "The Last Animal," a professor of zoology (at some unspecified time in the future) is despised by his academic colleagues who consider the study of animals to be backward and unprogressive. He finds himself in possession of the world's last animal, and at first he and his son are greatly excited. But neither of them know what to do with it. Eventually the animal bites the zoologist. The boy, who finds the animal boring, decides to punish it by neglect. Finally and hopelessly, the animal dies of starvation.

Perhaps the finest of these early stories is "In Prison" which appeared, long after it was written, in the *Partisan Review*.[5] It is a monologue in which the narrator, confronted with a world which seems to be chaotic, unprincipled and unhuman, forces upon himself a role which serves his own psychological need for order. Nature, soliloquizes the main character, intended him to live in prison. He looks forward passionately to being there. No voluntary, self-imposed incarceration can be the same, for choice implies that there are alternatives. An incontrovertible distinction that must be made is, he claims, between Choice and Necessity.

In the world, where choice is obligatory, freedom is inhibited by personal conscience and social expectations. But choice in prison is restricted and becomes possibility. Confusion is reduced to a dimension in which the finest esthetic distinctions can be made. So the narrator dwells upon the possible shapes and colors of his cell with greedy anticipation. He imagines that in prison he will be able to distinguish himself in matters of dress, for the slightest variation in his appearance will set him apart from the other prisoners. He will limit his reading to a single, dull, incomprehensible book which he will then feel free to interpret without having to labor within the bondage of the author's intentions.

At the end of the story is a key passage in which the narrator, having confessed to an inability to succeed "at large" in the world, rejoices in a Hegelian philosophy. Freedom is knowledge of Necessity; he believes nothing else as ardently. It becomes at once clear that the position of the prisoner is very like that of the man who sleeps on top of the mast. The prisoner is convinced that he can live in the world only if he does not know what it is. It is as "necessary" for him to live in prison as it is for the unbeliever to keep his eyes shut. To live with the truth—to be sensible of more than the mind can accept—is to be plunged into anonymity and chaos. It is to fall into the sea which is "hard as diamonds" and "wants to destroy us all."

"In Prison" belongs to a genre of quasi-philosophical fantasy which includes Poe's tales of horror and perhaps the novels of Kafka and Dostoevsky. While Miss Bishop's story is eerily convincing, it (like "The Unbeliever") has an air of being not quite serious. Yet it is not a parody of the genre, for it is curiously compelling and very probably has some bearing on Elizabeth Bishop's own feelings about life and art. Its lightness prevents it from being lugubrious and overly grotesque, but its theme is serious.

VI

Elizabeth Bishop has written once or twice of the dreamy state of consciousness she lived in while she was a student at Vassar. Yet she has never been afraid of the physical world. Rather, she has taken refuge in it by walking, sailing, swimming, and fishing—by priding herself on her ability to "do things" after her secluded, sickly childhood.

Throughout her life she has been an inveterate traveler. In the summer of 1932 she and a college classmate made a walking tour of Newfoundland, at that time a primitive, unknown region of North America. After her graduation from Vassar in 1934, she lived briefly in New York City before she went to Europe in 1935. There, she lived principally in Paris but made long excursions to England, North Africa, and Spain. One summer she spent in Brittany, living alone in a remote farmhouse where, she remembers, she read in French and with great excitement the poetry of Rimbaud. Returning to the United States in 1936, she spent a winter on the West Coast of Florida. At this time she went on a fishing trip to Key West and decided to return later to live there. That summer she went to Ireland, London, Italy, and then back to Paris for six months. In 1938 she moved to Key West where she lived, off and on, until she went to Mexico in 1943. It was not until 1945 that she published her first book of poems, *North & South*.

Nearly all the poems in her first book are, as we might expect, connected with her travels. Yet they are not really travel poems; they are not about famous places or even great works of art. They are concerned instead with Miss Bishop's own sense of place. They present a view of the world as it appears to her— not a social phenomenon but a set of visible surfaces which, in their shifting relationships, sometimes reveal momentarily, obliquely, a kind of truth or a transcendent beauty and harmony which arises out of and somehow balances the chaos of experience.

There is something in poems like "The Monument," "The Map," and "The Imaginary Iceberg" (all discussed in detail in later chapters) which suggests the abstract objectivism of Wallace Stevens. But, unlike Stevens, Miss Bishop has never felt obliged to define her metaphysical ideas or to defend, in the abstract, the terms of her vision. Often, too, her poems contain a trace of nineteenth-century disillusionment that is expressed, of course, without Victorian mannerisms but that echoes, for all their contemporaneity of diction, something of the wistfulness of A. E. Housman and even of Matthew Arnold. The poem "Chemin de Fer," for example, concludes with these despairing quatrains:

> The hermit shot off his shot-gun
> and the tree by the cabin shook.
> Over the pond went a ripple.
> The pet hen went chook-chook.
>
> "Love should be put into action!"
> screamed the old hermit.
> Across the pond an echo
> tried and tried to confirm it.

There is a note of pathos, too, at the end of the long travel poem (which did not appear until Elizabeth Bishop's second book was published in 1955) entitled "Over 2,000 Illustrations and a Complete Concordance." After a description of her own amorphous and vaguely dissatisfying travels, the poem breaks, almost rhetorically, into a lamentation for the lost synthesis of innocence represented by an illustration in an old concordance to the Bible:

> Everything connected by 'and' and 'and'!
> Open the book. (The gilt rubs off the edges
> of the pages and pollinates the fingertips.)
> Open the heavy book. Why couldn't we have seen
> this old nativity while we were at it?
> —the dark ajar, the rock breaking with light,
> and undisturbed, unbreathing flame,
> colorless, sparkless, freely fed on straw,
> and lulled within, a family with pets,
> —and looked and looked our infant sight away.

North & South was published just after the conclusion of World War II, but it has nothing to do with the war. The poems are not social, and Elizabeth Bishop herself considers that she belongs to the generation of poets which flourished after World War I. Most of *North & South* was written in the 1930's and first published in the *Partisan Review*. In style and tone the poems bear comparison with some of William Carlos Williams' and Marianne Moore's which were appearing at the same time. But the resemblance is only superficial. Elizabeth Bishop tends to be more conservative in matters of structure than Williams or Miss Moore.

Occasionally, like Miss Moore (whom she met during her last year at Vassar and with whom she has been friends ever since), Elizabeth Bishop has experimented with syllabic stanzas: she has regulated the form of her poems according to the number of syllables in each line instead of counting the number of beats. More often, though—as in "The Unbeliever"—she has been more interested in the shape of her poems on the page, in the sound of repetitive word patterns, and in rhymes. She is particularly a master of enjambment, and her sentences often flow effortlessly through the most demanding of stanza patterns, as, for instance, in this passage from "Roosters":

> In the morning
> a low light is floating
> in the backyard, and gilding
>
> from underneath
> the broccoli, leaf by leaf;
> how could the night have come to grief?
>
> gilding the tiny
> floating swallow's belly
> and lines of pink cloud in the sky,
>
> the day's preamble
> like wandering lines in marble. . . .

After 1946, when she received the Houghton Mifflin Poetry Award for *North & South*, Elizabeth Bishop was generally recognized in America as an important poet. She did not lead, nor has she ever led, an especially literary life. Her friendships with other writers, such as Randall Jarrell and Robert Lowell, have been personal. On the whole, her friends have affected her life more than her career as a poet. When she lived in Key West she met the philosopher John Dewey, whom she speaks of with affectionate admiration and to whose daughter Jane she dedicated the poem "A Cold Spring." Pauline Hemingway, the novelist's second wife, was another close friend—apparently humane, witty, and stoic, like Elizabeth Bishop herself. As for her feelings for Marianne Moore, they are plainly enough expressed in a panegyric written for her as a birthday offering. Although "Invitation to Miss Marianne Moore" is a pastiche of a serious poem by Pablo Neruda, its whimsical bravura is straight Bishop:

> From Brooklyn, over the Brooklyn Bridge, on this fine morning,
> please come flying
> In a cloud of fiery pale chemicals,
> please come flying,
> to the rapid rolling of thousands of small blue drums
> descending out of the mackerel sky
> over the glittering grandstand of harbor-water,
> please come flying . . .

The poem continues at some length in this vein, and there are some priceless lines, such as the following: "For whom the grim museums will behave/like courteous male bower-birds;/for whom the agreeable lions lie in wait/on the steps of the Public Library,/ eager to rise and follow through the doors; up into the reading rooms. . . ."

In 1949 Elizabeth Bishop was appointed Consultant in Poetry at the Library of Congress in Washington, and she moved to the capital. While living there, she, like many other poets at that time, often visited Ezra Pound at St. Elizabeth's Hospital. A poem, "Visits to St. Elizabeth's," published in the *Partisan Review* in 1950, summarizes, in that era of controversy over Pound, her extraordinarily balanced impression of him. He was, for her, a sadly paradoxical figure, tragically destroyed by himself and by his time, yet curiously victorious; he was at once heroic and pathetic.

Elizabeth Bishop was not happy in Washington. When in

1951 she was awarded a number of literary prizes, she decided to use her money to sail around South America. In November she set off, intending to stop in Rio de Janiero to visit friends before continuing on to the Straits of Magellan. Then, while in Brazil, she had a violent recurrence of the allergies she had suffered as a child—brought on this time from eating cashew fruit. She was forced to stay on in Rio for some months. Afterwards, when she had recovered, she found that she was enthralled by the spacious, brilliant, paradoxical Brazilian city, and she decided to make her home there.

Today Miss Bishop shares a beautiful modern house in Petrópolis with her friend Lota de Macedo Soares—a house that has become a center in Brazil for visiting artists and intellectuals. Elizabeth Bishop herself, however, is one of those rare women who are interested in ideas without giving the impression of being "intellectual." Modest and unassertive, she is reluctant to talk about herself; and, as in her poetry, she is absorbed by the things in the world about her rather than in self-analysis.

In the course of time her shyness has abated but her liking for travel has not. During the 1950's she made a number of trips to the United States where she still feels at home in New York City. In Brazil, however, repeated expeditions into the "interior" —many of them on the Amazon River—have nourished her imagination and provided a specific, geographical focus for her remarkable eye. She is, as always, indefatigably curious to explore the textures of her environment to which, like Keats, she responds with a "negative capability." She is able to see without wanting to make judgments, to investigate without having to fix her identity by taking sides. She is able, therefore, to live in the fierce political climate of Brazil without seeming to be affected by it. She is a poet whose imagination is excited by what Archibald MacLeish has called the "arable world"—the world of sensations, vision, appetite—to which power in a social sense is largely indifferent. The mind that apprehends this world

[47]

often slips through the coarser nets of faction and in some bewilderment wonders what all the fuss can be about.

Yet Elizabeth Bishop is not naive. Unlike Keats, for whom things of natural beauty in a still sparsely populated England *could* seem to be eternal, her arable world, even in Brazil, is under continual threat. The protective, almost moralizing tone of some of her recent poetry probably reflects her passionate commitment to the natural world which is disappearing as civilization spreads. A poem published in the *New Yorker* in 1957 describes an armadillo's retreat from a forest fire, and ends in this fanfare of italics and exclamation points:

> *Too pretty, dreamlike mimicry!*
> *O falling fire and piercing cry*
> *and panic, and a weak mailed fist*
> *clenched ignorant against the sky!*

Compare this ending with the conclusion of "The Fish" in which the personal emotions of the poet are suppressed by the imagery until the very last line when, with utmost simplicity, they are released, clarifying and giving resonance to the whole poem.

Perhaps it is a natural corollary to Elizabeth Bishop's increasing maturity and empathetic awareness that there should be a slackening now of her early genius—unequaled by any American poet writing today—for creating pure, resonant images. It is only reasonable to suppose that life has become less mystifying (and therefore expressable only in symbols) as it has become more acceptable to her. Moreover, the flood of "confessional" poetry that has recently appeared in the United States may have some extent broken down Elizabeth Bishop's natural reticence. Twenty years ago she would have been as incapable of the frank simplicity of "Manners" as of the near-sentimentalism of "First Death in Nova Scotia":

> Arthur was very small.
> He was all white like a doll
> that hasn't been painted yet.

Jack Frost had started to paint him
the way he always painted
the Maple Leaf (Forever).
He had just begun on his hair,
a few red strokes, and then
Jack Frost had dropped the brush
and left him white forever.

It would be wrong to conclude, however, that Elizabeth Bishop's poetry has obediently changed with the fashions or that she is now any less capable of original perceptions than when she was younger. It is much more likely that her early poems were written in a state of near somnambulism: that she *knew* less about the world and therefore could *see* more of it. If this is the case, then she may have a great deal more poetry to write. She is interested in abstract painting, and it may be that she will be able to evolve a comparable abstract poetry, not, perhaps, like the near-Surrealism of "The Unbeliever," but more a calculated and "intellectual" abstractionism such as Christopher Middleton, among others, is writing now in England.

The kind of poetry Elizabeth Bishop writes at her best—a style of poetry which owes as much to the French poets Apollinaire and Laforgue as it does to Wallace Stevens, Marianne Moore and other American poets of her generation— is not now in vogue in the United States. In recent years there has been a reaction against formality, emotional restraint, and humor among American poets; what particularly characterizes the poetry of the 1960's is its intense and very personal seriousness.

Yet, in spite of her love of conceits, of her personal reticence, of her tendency to laugh at the very things she takes most seriously, Elizabeth Bishop is among the few American poets writing today who has been able to say something uniquely true about the way modern life is experienced. At moments she has been able to divorce herself from habitual modes of interpretation and to receive sensations independently of her predis-

[49]

ELIZABETH BISHOP

position to judge them. That is, the sensations themselves have been questionable; they could mean one thing, they could mean another. And because there is doubt about the meaning of everything, Elizabeth Bishop refuses to settle for any comprehensive philosophy. She does not offer any consoling answers, but she does *show* us that the world can be accepted and even enjoyed without answers. For her, the world is, in spite of its terrible confusions and injustices, a rich one, and in her poems she repeatedly strikes a clear, unwavering note of personal acceptance.

CHAPTER **2**

The Artist

IT WILL BE OBVIOUS to anyone who has even an anthology acquaintance with Elizabeth Bishop that she is a poet who lives in a painter's world in which shapes and colors are enormously significant and in which the meaning of experience is inextricably connected with the appearance of it. Language, for her, is primarily a means of description (although it is not only that); and yet she seldom uses it impressionistically, as Wallace Stevens did, but with an attention to the particular and the definite which makes her poetry both more traditional and more realistic than his. In her long, descriptive poems, particularly, there are passages which are so exact that they seem to strain to be poetry at all. Take, for example, these lines from "At the Fishhouses":

> The big fish tubs are completely lined
> with layers of beautiful herring scales
> and the wheelbarrows are similarly plastered
> with creamy iridescent coats of mail,
> with small iridescent flies crawling on them.
> Up on the little slope behind the houses,
> set in the sparse bright sprinkle of grass,
> is an ancient wooden capstan,
> cracked, with two long bleached handles
> and some melancholy stains, like dried blood,
> where the ironwork has rusted.

It is misleading, of course, to quote such a passage in isolation; for this description is part of a long poem to which the details contribute more than the sum of its parts. Nevertheless, Miss Bishop is less willing than most visual poets—than William Carlos Williams or Wallace Stevens—to blur the edges of her verbal canvases. She is careful not to confuse the perceptions of her readers while she confronts them with attitudes which are often more than sense perceptions.

For this reason, many images in her poems bear comparison with the realistic surrealism of the Maine painter, Andrew Wyeth.[1] They give the same impression of outward simplicity; they have the same severe, puritanical starkness; they are equally preoccupied with the surfaces of things and with what can be suggested by a selection and presentation of surfaces. Even in her choice of subject matter, Miss Bishop is like Mr. Wyeth. She has drawn repeatedly upon her feeling for the sea and coastline, and the figures in her poems are, like his, natural and unsophisticated people whose lives contrast with nature but never violate it. This characteristic can best be observed in a poem like "Jerónimo's House" in which the poet's point of view emerges out of an abundance of detail:

My house, my fairy
   palace, is
of perishable
   clapboards with
three rooms in all,
   my grey wasps' nest
of chewed-up paper
   glued with spit.

My home, my love-nest,
   is endowed
with a veranda
   of wooden lace,
adorned with ferns
   planted in sponges,
and the front room
   with red and green

left-over Christmas
   decorations
looped from the corners
   to the middle
above my little
   center table
of woven wicker
   painted blue,

and four blue chairs
   and an affair
for the smallest baby
   with a tray
with ten big beads.
   Then on the walls
two palm-leaf fans
   and a calendar

and on the table
  one fried fish
spattered with burning
  scarlet sauce,
a little dish
  of hominy grits
and four pink tissue-
  paper roses.

Also I have
  hung on a hook,
an old French horn
  repainted with
aluminum paint.
  I play each year
in the parade
  for José Marti.

At night you'd think
  my house abandoned.
Come closer. You
  can see and hear
the writing-paper
  lines of light
and the voices of
  my radio

singing flamencos
  in between
the lottery numbers.
  When I move
I take these things,
  not much more, from
my shelter from
  the hurricane.

It is abundantly evident that this is not Jerónimo's poem but Elizabeth Bishop's. The selection of the character, the description of the house, the metaphorical and gently ironical implications of "fairy palace" at the beginning and "hurricane" at the end—all these particulars which so rightly fit the mood and tone and which, for this reason, we are likely to take for granted, are actually the means by which the poet expresses an attitude of her own.

We notice that it is an attitude rather than an opinion, a suggestion rather than a statement. While the poet is aware that to Jerónimo this poor little house is a "fairy palace," a "love-nest," a beautiful, precious, invulnerable refuge from a chaos whose nature he fears and whose power he refuses to think about, she sees that the house in reality is as frail as the paper it is made of. Jerónimo's house is an absurd, impermanent, precarious bastion against, not the inhuman but, far worse, the *unhuman* forces of nature. And these forces reduce all human shelters against them to a level absurdity. Are we, with our skyscrapers and highways any more secure than Jerónimo? This question is implied in the poem, and the negative answer makes "Jerónimo's House" in its quiet way terrifying. From unhuman nature there is no escape; there are only alternative illusions of safety.

"The Fish" is a more ambitious poem than "Jerónimo's House," but its effect is similar. Pictorial, lucid, extremely detailed, its simplicity is again deceptive. The poet has caught a huge fish and is looking at him as he hangs helplessly outside her boat. All the details of the fish's appearance—his skin hanging in strips "like ancient wallpaper," his gills, his eyes, his bones "and coarse white flesh/packed in like feathers" and "the dramatic reds and blacks of his shiny entrails"—everything which might appear disgusting or ugly or simply uninteresting to a less perceptive observer—bears in upon the poet's consciousness and leads to the moment when she notices that

> from his lower lip
> —if you could call it a lip—
> grim, wet, and weapon-like,
> hung five old pieces of fish-line,
> or four and a wire leader
> with the swivel still attached,
> with all their five big hooks
> grown firmly in his mouth.
> A green line, frayed at the end
> where he broke it, two heavier lines,
> and a fine black thread
> still crimped from the strain and snap
> when it broke and he got away.
> Like medals with their ribbons
> frayed and wavering,
> a five-haired beard of wisdom
> trailing from his aching jaw.

In the course of the poet's observations she has suddenly "seen" the fish—recognized its power and beauty and the enormous majesty of its indifference. And at this moment it becomes evident that the poem is not only about a fish but about the poet looking at the fish. The fish is victorious because the

poet, too, is victorious. It is the poet who has been able, through
her absolute integrity of observation, to rise above what D. H.
Lawrence might have called "a pettiness":

> I stared and stared
> and victory filled up
> the little rented boat,
> from the pool of bilge
> where oil had spread a rainbow
> around the rusted engine
> to the bailer rusted orange,
> the sun-cracked thwarts,
> the oarlocks on their strings,
> the gunnels—until everything
> was rainbow, rainbow, rainbow!
> And I let the fish go.

It is a testimony to Miss Bishop's strength and sensitivity
that the end, the revelation or "moment of truth," is described
with the same attention to detail as the rest of the poem. The
temptation might have been to float off into an airy apotheosis,
but Miss Bishop stays right in the boat with the engine and the
bailer. Because she does so, she is able to use words like "victory"
and "rainbow" without fear of triteness and to be explicit about
her experience without becoming florid or ecstatic. To say simply
all that is meant, to describe without either avoiding or depending upon the normal associations of words, to be "artlessly
rhetorical," as Miss Bishop puts it in another poem—are not these
objectives that many a poet "would give his eyes for"? In
"The Fish" Elizabeth Bishop seems effortlessly to have achieved
them.

Miss Bishop's descriptions are not usually so bare, so free of
metaphor and simile as these passages suggest. Most of her
images, even in "The Fish", are comparative:

> Here and there
> his brown skin hung in strips
> like ancient wall paper. . . .

I looked into his eyes
which were far larger than mine
but shallower and yellowed
the irises backed and packed
with tarnished tinfoil
seen through the lenses
of old scratched isinglass.

Any poet, no matter how concerned with visible surfaces, has
an advantage over a painter (although it is not always handled
as if it were an advantage) in that, within the conventions of
his art, he is able to describe two or more things at once: fish
skin and wall paper; fish eyes and tinfoil under isinglass. In "The
Fish," as in other poems, Elizabeth Bishop's command of
metaphor is sophisticated but accurate. She makes no concessions
to accepted clichés, preferring to see for herself. Yet, on the other
hand, she rarely forces her comparisons beyond the limits of
credibility. At her best she is capable of using them very
delicately and suggestively: "The little white churches have
been dropped into the matted hills/like lost quartz arrowheads."
or "The frowsy sponge boats keep coming in/with the obliging
air of retrievers."

When she writes in this easy, conversational vein, few possibilities for comparison elude her assimilative eye, just as few
details of the setting escape her immediate one. Most of her long,
realistic poems such as "Florida," "A Cold Spring," "The Bight,"
"Cape Breton," and "At the Fishhouses" are no more—and no
less—than extremely perceptive, beautifully executed evocations
of places *and*, inseparable from them, the feelings Miss Bishop
has had about them. Because she has been able to describe her
feelings precisely, her poems are personal. For what this artist
explores is not the nature of external existence itself, but the
connection between apparent existence and how she interprets
it. In one sense, indeed, completely objective writing is impossible. Although a work of art may not necessarily be about

human consciousness, it always pertains to it and so we can say that any work of art is an interpretation.

II

We have so far been discussing Elizabeth Bishop as if she were a traditional New England Realist. This, in some measure, she is. But there is another side to her poetry. It derives from the same acute sensitivity to the world about her, but its outlook is modern and European; and our first impression is that this poetry contrasts rather strangely with the severe simplicity of poems like "The Fish."

There is a temptation to exaggerate the importance of newness in art of the twentieth century, and certainly a great deal of pretentious nonsense has been produced in the name of "modernity." On the other hand, it would be absurd to pretend that Europe in general and Paris and Vienna in particular did not give the Western world a new idea of the possibilities of art in the period roughly between 1890 and 1940. Whatever we may think of modern theories, it is difficult to imagine any serious future painting that does not recognize the significance of Cubism and Surrealism, just as it is impossible to conceive of a future music that does not take into account Schoenberg's and Webern's explorations of structures free from tonality. The experiments with language were perhaps more temporary, and yet James Joyce and Gertrude Stein (not to mention French *avant-garde* writers such as André Breton and, later, Alain Robbe-Grillet) were testing language as a medium for art at the same time that the philosopher Ludwig Wittgenstein was demonstrating its possibilities and limitations for systematic analysis.

The early twentieth century was, we hardly need point out, a time of great intellectual disturbance—one that many writers of the nineteenth century had anticipated but which never took over the mainstream of art until after Baudelaire, Rimbaud, and Kafka. The modernist or Surrealist-like (not Surrealist) poems of Elizabeth Bishop can only be fully appreciated if we understand something of what the intellectual atmosphere was like during the time she was at Vassar—an atmosphere which, when she later went to Paris, prevailed among the artists who were then most fashionable.

The general state of mind that gave birth to the modern outlook in art is so well described by Professor Eric Heller in his introduction to his study of Thomas Mann that I can do no better than quote from it. In discussing Hofmannsthal's imaginary letter from an Elizabethan nobleman named Lord Chandos, Professor Heller writes that this letter

> is more than a self-revelation of Hofmannsthal; it reflects a deep disturbance of the age [the 1890's] itself, at least in so far as it is presented by its literature. This is how Hofmannsthal describes the disturbance. The traditional order of things fall apart, and their meanings lie buried under the fragments. Elements, once bound together to make a world, now present themselves to the poet in monstrous separateness. To speak of them coherently at all would be to speak untruthfully. The commonplace phrases of the daily round of observations seem all of a sudden insoluble riddles. "My mind," he writes, "compelled me to view all things with uncanny closeness; and just as I once saw a piece of skin from my little finger under a magnifying lens, and it looked like a landscape with mighty furrows and caves, so it was now with people and what they said and did. I failed to see it with the simplifying eye of habit and custom."[2]

The failure to see with the simplifying eye of habit and custom plunged Hofmannsthal into blackness and nihilism. But for other artists this release from tradition was a source of a tremendous sense of freedom. What perhaps was most characteristic of early modern art—what bound the arts together (as they are not bound now) and gave them an almost messianic seriousness—was their overwhelming need to define new concepts of reality.[3] Unsatisfactory philosophies, unsatisfactory moral codes, and unsatisfactory artistic "rules" not only could

[58]

but had to be abolished; and excitable innovators, like Guillaume Apollinaire who liked to be in the vanguard of new movements, were wildly optimistic. In an address delivered at the Théâtre du Vieux Colombier in 1917, Apollinaire frantically hailed *l'esprit nouveau* of poetry which was to become the partner of science in the opening up of the new world. The new art, he proclaimed, "is not a decorative art, nor is it an impressionistic art. It is entirely devoted to the study of external and internal nature; it is entirely consecrated to the truth."[4]

Yet, there was difficulty which Apollinaire and his friends did not anticipate. The artist's conception of the truth which was to be revealed by a study of "external and internal nature" did not correspond to the idea of truth which was emerging in the sciences. The ultimate reality which the Surrealists, among others, wished to free from the bondages of appearance was becoming, in physics as well as in psychology, less and less of a scientific certainty. As the twentieth century progressed, the artist, instead of finding an ally in science, found that its ends as well as its means were hostile to his optimistic vision of a truth which trancended the world of experience.

To many artists, art itself was an object of worship. Form, beauty, and emotion seemed to be the only certain truths in a world in which humanity was diminished and humiliated. So it was that Paul Valéry, writing in 1937 of his youth in Paris at the turn of the century, looked back with nostalgia and disappointment to a time when art was a kind of "essential nourishment impossible to forgo."[5] Other artists, taking over, with adjustments, the theories of Freud and Jung, regarded the subconscious as the only source of reality. The Surrealist painter, Giorgio di Chirico, for instance, rejected rationality altogether.

"A work of art must escape all human limits," di Chirico wrote; "Logic and common sense will only interfere. But once these barriers are broken, it will enter the regions of childhood vision and dream. . . ." Again, writing of the mystery of creation, sen-

sible of all the irrational aspects of it, he concluded in the manner of Hegel that "Everything has two aspects: the current
aspect which we see nearly always and which ordinary men see
and the ghostly and metaphysical aspect which only rare indi-
viduals may see in moments of clairvoyance and metaphysical
abstraction."[6]

III

Elizabeth Bishop came to Paris when Surrealism was popular
among artists, and it is certain that it influenced her a great
deal. Like most sensitive, imaginative people, she had lived a
great deal in a dream world not unlike that which di Chirico
describes. She did not need Surrealism to show her that this
world was indeed real—real in the sense that it could be experienced by the imagination. Yet there was something too practical and common-sensical in her make-up (the New England
Yankee side of her character, perhaps) which prevented her
from surrendering wholly to dreams. All her life she has been
aware of both worlds—of the rational and the extra-rational, of
the everyday and the dream. The tension, or contradiction, that √
she has felt to exist between them is considerable; and, because
she has refused to relinquish either one, the problem of reality
has been an especially obsessive one for her.

Elizabeth Bishop has had one advantage, however, which has
preserved her in the maelstrom of contemporary spiritual struggles. Most of the time she has been able to laugh at the whole
predicament—not harshly, not sardonically, but gaily. For example, we compare the view of existence put forth in "A
Miracle for Breakfast" (an accomplished sestina) with that
described by Hofmannsthal in his letter. The vision of fragmentation and of an essentially malleable universe is the same.
Everything we see, as Wittgenstein once remarked, could be
otherwise. Yet for Elizabeth Bishop this perception is not a
threatening one; it actually gives her grounds for hope. In this
whimsical but not unprofound series of images in "A Miracle"
we are offered not a negation but a moral affirmation:

At six o'clock we were waiting for coffee,
waiting for coffee and the charitable crumb
that was going to be served from a certain balcony.
—like kings of old, or like a miracle.
It was still dark. One foot of the sun
steadied itself on a long ripple in the river.

The first ferry of the day had just crossed the river.
It was so cold we hoped that the coffee
would be very hot, seeing that the sun
was not going to warm us; and that the crumb
would be a loaf each, buttered, by a miracle.
At seven a man stepped out on the balcony.

He stood for a minute alone on the balcony
looking over our heads toward the river.
A servant handed him the makings of a miracle,
consisting of one lone cup of coffee
and one roll, which he proceeded to crumb,
his head, so to speak, in the clouds—along with the sun.

Was the man crazy? What under the sun
was he trying to do, up there on his balcony!
Each man received one rather hard crumb,
which some flicked scornfully into the river,
and, in a cup, one drop of the coffee.
Some of us stood around, waiting for the miracle.

I can tell what I saw next; it was not a miracle.
A beautiful villa stood in the sun
and from its doors came the smell of hot coffee.
In front, a baroque white plaster balcony
added by birds, who nest along the river,
—I saw it with one eye close to the crumb—

and galleries and marble chambers. My crumb
my mansion, made for me by a miracle,
through ages, by insects, birds, and the river
working the stone. Every day, in the sun,
at breakfast time I sit on my balcony
with my feet up, and drink gallons of coffee.

We licked up the crumb and swallowed the coffee.
A window across the river caught the sun
as if the miracle were working on the wrong balcony.

This poem can perhaps be taken as a parable; as a modern version of Christ's feeding of the ten thousand or as a variation on the ceremony of the Eucharist. Elizabeth Bishop herself claims that she had neither of these ideas in mind when she wrote it, but that is no proof, of course, that they are not there. But whatever the Christian implication, surely the moral one is obvious: to each of us is given the makings of a "miracle"—the simple elements of life made "though ages, by insects, birds, and the river/working the stone." The natural, not the supernatural, miracle is what we must expect; happiness consists of knowing and living with what one has. Put like this, the sentiment is banal; but the poem is not. It is amusing, delightful, intriguing. Because the coffee and the crumb are homely images, they parody the "high thinking" behind the moral. Yet they are appropriate because the poem concerns homely things. The crumb that becomes a mansion (like Jerónimo's "fairy palace") becomes so because it is *seen* close to the eye—just as Hofmannsthal's skin became a terrifying landscape of furrows and caves because it was *seen* under a microscope. And what is the reality? It is, of course, what we make of it; how we interpret it.

Miss Bishop's poems are gay, but they are stoical. What they affirm is that nothing can be affirmed beyond what can be known through observation. Because of this, observation is very important. In "Cirque d'Hiver" the details are realistic, not imaginary as in "A Miracle for Breakfast"; but again looking is the test of thinking:

> Across the floor flits the mechanical toy,
> fit for a king of several centuries back.
> A little circus horse with real white hair.
> His eyes are glossy black.
> He bears a little dancer on his back.
>
> She stands upon her toes and turns and turns.
> A slanting spray of artificial roses
> is stitched across her skirt and tinsel bodice.
> Above her head she poses
> another spray of artificial roses.

His mane and tail are straight from Chirico.
He has a formal, melancholy soul.
He feels her pink toes dangle toward his back
along the little pole
that pierces both her body and her soul

and goes through his, and reappears below,
under his belly, as a big tin key.
He canters three steps, then he makes a bow,
canters again, bows on one knee,
canters, then clicks and stops, and looks at me.

The dancer, by this time, has turned her back.
He is the more intelligent by far.
Facing each other rather desperately—
his eye is like a star—
we stare and say, "Well, we have come this far."

In "Cirque d'Hiver" the seriousness of tone provided by the formal, rhyming verses is amusingly at odds with an apparently trivial incident. Ordinarily we would expect a poem like this to collect itself into a moral at the end. Whimsy and seriousness usually combine for the purposes of parable or satire as in the fables of Aesop and La Fontaine or as the disingenuous innocence of Jonathan Swift's *Gulliver's Travels*. In "Cirque d'Hiver" there is a sort of moral, but it is not exactly what we expect. Instead of telling us what we ought or ought not to do or believe, the poem leaves us with a rather stark condolence. The little horse is no better off than we are; each of us partakes of the unknown. If we wonder whether the poet wishes to leave us with a cosmic or simply a comic view of ourselves, the answer is surely with both. The cosmic and the comic are identical —just as the body and the soul of the little dancer are identical. Everything, human and mechanical is, in a sense, equal; point of view is the only criterion of distinction. And point of view is by definition relative.

"Cirque d'Hiver" is a clever, perceptive, and—in spite of (or because of) the irony of the ending—humorous poem. "The Gentleman of Shalott" is more humorous still. Again, its inspiration is visual. A play on the bilateral symmetry of human anatomy, the poem is at the same time a spoof of Tennysonian Romanticism and a satire on modern man's preoccupation with split personality. Readers of Tennyson's poem will remember that the Lady of Shalott's mirror shattered, betokening her death, when she exchanged its unreal vision of Sir Launcelot for a real view of him through her window. The Gentleman of Shalott is equally dependent on a mirror for existence, but in his case the mirror runs down his spine, dividing his body in half. It is with the implications of this division of personality that the poem deals; the question for him is not only one of reality and unreality but of the very modern concept of self-identity:

> Which eye's his eye?
> Which limb lies
> next the mirror?
> For neither is clearer
> nor a different color
> than the other,
> nor meets a stranger
> in this arrangement
> of leg and leg and
> arm and so on.
> To his mind
> it's the indication
> of a mirrored reflection
> somewhere along the line
> of what we call the spine.
>
> He felt in modesty
> his person was
> half looking-glass,
> for why should he
> be doubled?
> The glass must stretch down
> down his middle,
> or rather down the edge.
> But he's in doubt
> as to which side's in or out
> or the mirror.

There's little margin for error,
but there's no proof either.
And if half his head's reflected,
thought, he thinks, might be affected.

But he's resigned
to such economical design.
If the glass slips
he's in a fix—
only one leg, etc. But
while it stays put
he can walk and run
and his hands can clasp one
another. The uncertainty
he says he
finds exhilarating. He loves
that sense of constant re-adjustment.
He wishes to be quoted as saying at present:
"Half is enough."

The poem is the more comical because the Gentleman is a modest man who only *supposes* that his person is half looking glass; he can't imagine why *he* should be doubled. The dilemma, then, is probably imaginary. Nevertheless, it is a worrisome one; and his sense of uneasiness is evident even as he claims to find the uncertainty "exhilarating."

We are in the habit of expecting that a poem whose theme is man's self-doubt, hypocrisy, and endemic sense of schizophrenia will be, however amusing, essentially resentful, as the satirical dramas of Ionesco are resentful or as the poems of Cummings and Eliot are bitter-whimsical. In comparison, "The Gentleman of Shalott" seems light. Its irony is essentially *dégagé*. The poet does not seem to be setting forth a message or even, until we examine the implications of the poem closely, to be offering a criticism.

This effect of disinterestedness is wholly original. As we have seen, for Elizabeth Bishop, the picture, the image, the formal arrangement of words and rhymes in a poem exactly balance the emotional elements. Unlike Marianne Moore, she has not, on the whole, tried to invent new forms. She has found traditional typography and structures satisfactory, has developed them in her own way, and has trusted to her ear and her eye for the rest. Her free verse seems to come as naturally as possible and does not strain to be novel.

IV

Yet in spite of the gay tone of her work, the experience of art, like that of life itself, is a serious one for her. The question of reality is one, in fact, that she tries to resolve through art; for art, for Elizabeth Bishop, is neither an end, a truth that must be worshiped in a disintegrating society, nor is it really a means to such an end. One suspects that Elizabeth Bishop does not expect to achieve such an end. Art, for her, is rather a means of making life bearable—of making it comprehensible and more meaningful than it normally seems. It is also more: it is a way of reconciling the two worlds of reality which Miss Bishop has experienced, of momentarily bringing together rationality and irrationality into a sustained and even mystical but never unbelievable whole. But it is best to let Miss Bishop speak for herself. In a letter to me in which she discusses, among other things, the role of consciousness and subconsciousness in art, she writes:

There is no "split." Dreams, works of art (some) glimpses of the always-more-successful surrealism of everyday life, unexpected moments of empathy (is it?), catch a peripheral vision of whatever it is one can never really see full-face but that seems enormously important. I can't believe we are wholly irrational—and I do admire Darwin—But reading Darwin one admires the beautiful solid case being built up out of his endless, heroic observations, almost unconscious or automatic—and then comes a sudden relaxation, a forgetful phrase, and one feels that strangeness of his undertaking, sees the lonely young man, his eyes fixed on facts and minute details, sinking or sliding giddily off into the unknown. What one seems to want in art, in experiencing it, is the same thing that is necessary for its creation, a self-forgetful, perfectly useless concentration.

Although, as she says, there is no "split," Miss Bishop often attempts to reconcile psychic and physical experiences by treating them as if they were inversions or even correctives of each other. Such an inversion appears in the first stanza of "Sleeping Standing Up," a poem which poses the whole sleeping-waking paradox as if it were a fairy tale (and which also at the end shows us a dream world that is essentially a source of frustration):

> As we lie down to sleep the world turns half away
> through ninety dark degrees;
> the bureau lies on the wall
> and thoughts that were recumbent in the day
> rise as the others fall,
> stand up and make a forest of thick-set trees. . . .

Likewise in the wistful, song-like "Insomnia" (one of the very few love poems in her book) the moon in the bureau mirror seems to look into a world "inverted"

> where the left is always right
> where the shadows are really the body,
> where we stay awake all night,
> where the heavens are shallow as the sea
> is now deep, and you love me.

More spectacular is the long and rather difficult poem entitled "Love Lies Sleeping" in which there seems to be a revelation of the truer vision of an unconscious (or dead) man. The first eleven stanzas describe, with Miss Bishop's customary attention to detail, the coming of dawn over New York City:

> The cloud of smoke moves off.
> A shirt is taken off a thread-like clothes line;
>   Along the street below
> the water-wagon comes
> throwing its hissing, showy fan across
> peelings and newspapers.

Then, at the end, there are four stanzas which can be understood
as a rhetorical injunction addressed to the "cupids"—the driving
desires and impulses, perhaps—of the people who are getting up
and going to work:

> Queer cupids of all persons getting up
> whose evening meal they will prepare all day,
> you will dine well
> on his heart, on his and his,
>
> so send them about your business affectionately,
> dragging in the streets their unique loves.
> Scourge them with roses only,
> be light as helium,
>
> for always to one, or several, morning comes
> whose head has fallen over the edge of his bed,
> whose face is turned
> so that the image of
>
> the city grows down into his open eyes
> inverted and distorted. No. I mean
> distorted and revealed,
> if he sees it at all.

In contrast to the poems in which Elizabeth Bishop seems to
regard waking consciousness and dream experience as inversions of each other, there are poems in which the whole of experience is seen as a continuum. In "The Monument" there is
suggestion of the unknown and inexplicable—"the always-more-
successful surrealism"—which is present in both worlds but
visible only at "unexpected moments of empathy"—visible but
perhaps understandable only as symbols. "The Monument" is,
like "The Fish," a symbolic image; but it is an abstract one for
all that it is described with great attention to particulars. No
longer like a figure in a landscape by Andrew Wyeth, it resembles the wood rubbing of Max Ernst, which in fact inspired
the poem:[7]

THE MONUMENT

Now can you see the monument? It is of wood
built somewhat like a box. No. Built
like several boxes in descending sizes
one above the other.
Each is turned half-way round so that
its corners point toward the sides
of the one below and the angles alternate.
Then on the topmost cube is set
a sort of fleur-de-lys of weathered wood,
long petals of board, pierced with odd holes,
foursided, stiff, ecclesiastical.
From it four thin, warped poles spring out,
(slanted like fishing-poles or flag poles)
and from the jig-saw work hangs down,
four lines of vaguely whittled ornament
over the edges of the boxes
to the ground.
The monument is one-third set against
a sea; two-thirds against a sky.
The view is geared
(that is, the view's perspective)
so low there is no "far away,"
and we are far away within the view.
A sea of narrow, horizontal boards
lies out behind our lonely monument,
its long grains alternating right and left
like floor-boards—spotted, swarming-still,
and motionless. A sky runs parallel
and it is palings, coarser than the sea's:
splintery sunlight, and long fibred clouds.
"Why does that strange sea make no sound?
Is it because we're far away?
Where are we? Are we in Asia Minor,
or in Mongolia?"
                    An ancient promontory,
and ancient principality whose artist-prince
might have wanted to build a monument
to mark a tomb or boundary, or make
a melancholy or romantic scene of it . . .

"But that queer sea looks made of wood,
half-shining, like a driftwood sea.
And the sky looks wooden, grained with cloud.
It's like a stage-set; it is all so flat!
Those clouds are full of glistening splinters!
What is that?"
                    It is the monument.
"It's piled-up boxes,
outlined with shoddy fret-work, half-fallen off,
cracked and unpainted. It looks old."
—The strong sunlight, the wind from the sea,
all the conditions of its existence,
may have flaked off the paint, if ever it was painted,
and made it homelier than it was.
"Why did you bring me there to see it?
A temple of crates in cramped and crated scenery.
what can it prove?
I am tired of breathing this eroded air,
this dryness in which the monument is cracking."
It is an artifact
of wood. Wood holds together better
than sea or cloud or sand could by itself,
much better than real sea or sand or cloud.
It chose that way to grow and not to move.
The monument's an object, yet those decorations,
carelessly nailed, looking like nothing at all,
give it away as having life, and wishing;
wanting to be a monument, to cherish something.
The crudest scroll-work says "commemorate,"
while once each day the light goes around it
like a prowling animal,
or the rain falls on it, or the wind blows into it.
It may be solid, may be hollow.
The bones of the artist-prince may be inside
or far away on even dryer soil.
But roughly but adequately it can shelter
what is within (which after all
cannot have been intended to be seen.)
It is the beginning of a painting,
a piece of sculpture, or poem, or monument,
and all of wood. Watch it closely.

[70]

To offer a definitive analysis of a poem like this would of course be presumptuous. The image of the monument is what psychologists have sometimes called "overdetermined." The power of such an image or symbol, as Arnold Hauser observed in his study of the psychology and sociology of art, "lies in a multiplicity, a seeming inexhaustibility of meaning."[8] So the monument can stand for many things. It may represent the body of human achievement, the dry, eroded, crude yet precious remains of human history about which the sun goes "like a prowling animal" and upon which the indifferent rain beats and the wind blows. If we choose to understand it in this way, the monument appears to be a larger, more elaborate Jerónimo's house. The poem suggests that this monument of "piled up boxes/outlined with shoddy fret-work" is all that is left of the human past—is all that man can make to commemorate his evanescent triumphs in a ruthless, impersonal universe.

Again, the monument may represent the achievements of art. As "The Fish" is about the experience of life—about the possibility of moral triumph and victory—so "The Monument" may be about the experience of form, of an artistic order which is distinct from life yet expressive of it. In each poem the "perfectly useless concentration," the "case of solid observations," builds up to a point at which the poet "sails off into the unknown." In "The Fish" this moment occurs when the poet lets the fish go; in "The Monument" it occurs when the work of art becomes a justification of itself, when it begins to have a life of its own:

> But roughly but adequately it can shelter
> what is within (which after all
> cannot have been intended to be seen).
> It is the beginning of a painting,
> a piece of sculpture, or poem, or monument,
> and all of wood. Watch it closely.

If we do think of the monument as representing, in some manner, art or a work of art, then this is an art which is self-perpetuating and crude but at the same time incomprehensibly

associated with whatever it commemorates. Art is a barely satisfying memorial of life.

In "The Map" the question seems again to be that of the relationship between art and life (although it is a travesty of the
poem to put this so bluntly). The central and significant perception in "The Map," however, is that the map, while it
imitates the world it depicts, has a finer and more precise life of
its own. The map has all the qualities of balance and elegance
and beauty that the world lacks:

THE MAP

Land lies in water; it is shadowed green.
Shadows, or are they shallows, at its edges
showing the line of long sea-weeded ledges
where weeds hang to the simple blue from green.

Or does the land lean down to lift the sea from under,
drawing it unperturbed around itself?
Along the fine tan sandy shelf
is the land tugging at the sea from under?

The shadow of Newfoundland lies flat and still.
Labrador's yellow, where the moony Eskimo
has oiled it. We can stroke these lovely bays,
under a glass as if they were expected to blossom,
or as if to provide a clean cage for invisible fish.
The names of seashore towns run out to sea,
the names of cities cross the neighboring mountains
—the printer here experiencing the same excitement
as when emotion too far exceeds its cause.
These peninsulas take the water between thumb and finger
like women feeling for the smoothness of yard-goods.

Mapped waters are more quiet than the land is,
lending the land their waves' own conformation:
and Norway's hare runs south in agitation,
profiles investigate the sea, where land is.
Are they assigned, or can the countries pick their colors?
—What suit the character or the native waters best.
Topography displays no favorites; North's as near as West.
More delicate than the historians' are the map-makers' colors.

The Artist

The contradiction between what "The Monument" and "The Map" seem to say about the place of art in life can be resolved by a close reading of both poems. The monument can only "roughly but adequately" shelter what is within; the map, on the other hand, is a correction and a refinement of the world it represents. Surely both are accute observations. The world that art creates is, as Professor Hauser puts it, "a less chaotic, less confusing, more consistent form of existence."[9] But when we come to consider the adequacy of art for conveying a full picture of life's complexity, we see that it can only imperfectly do so. Art must falsify in order to simplify. It denies truth by isolating and refining it. And so we see that, with this distinction in mind, both poems are valid. Together, they give a fuller idea of what art is than either poem could alone.

Of course, "The Map" is also very much about a map—a real one that the poet once owned. It would be a pity to miss the descriptive nuances of this poem in a search for "inner meanings." Miss Bishop herself says that, while the monument was a "made-up" image and somewhat self-conscious for that reason (that is, she realized as she was writing it that it could mean many different things), the map and the iceberg (in the poem which is quoted below) were images which came to her in all innocence. She did not think of "symbolic meanings" for them until long afterwards.

Nevertheless, it is certain, too, that these poems *can* be interpreted symbolically. It is an enrichment to conceive of the iceberg in the following poem not only as an iceberg—which it patently is—but as a state of mind which gives rise to invention and creation. As the title suggests, it is an *imaginary* iceberg. It is that state of mind—visionary, and perhaps irrational or semi-rational—that we'd rather have than "the ship" or our ordinary, practical train of thought. The iceberg represents, in part at least, the creative imagination.

THE IMAGINARY ICEBERG

We'd rather have the iceberg than the ship,
although it meant the end of travel.
Although it stood stock-still like cloudy rock
and all the sea were moving marble.
We'd rather have the iceberg than the ship;
We'd rather own this breathing plain of snow
though the ship's sails were laid upon the sea
as the snow lies undissolved upon the water.
O solemn, floating field,
are you aware an iceberg takes repose
with you, and when it wakes may pasture on your snows?

This is a scene a sailor'd give his eyes for.
The ship's ignored. The iceberg rises
and sinks again; its glassy pinnacles
correct elliptics in the sky.
This is a scene where he who treads the boards
is artlessly rhetorical. The curtain
is light enough to rise on finest ropes
that airy twists of snow provide.
The wits of these white peaks
spar with the sun. Its weight the iceberg dares
upon a shifting stage and stands and stares.

This iceberg cuts its facets from within.
Like jewelry from a grave
it saves itself perpetually and adorns
only itself, perhaps the snows
which so surprise us lying on the sea.
Good-bye, we say, good-bye, the ship steers off
where waves give in to one anothers waves
and clouds run in a warmer sky.
Icebergs behoove the soul
(Both being self-made from elements least visible)
to see them so: fleshed, fair, erected indivisible.

It is also possible to interpret the imaginary iceberg as being
in some measure another description of Miss Bishop's conception of art. Like the map, the iceberg has a self-contained per-

fection of its own. Like the monument, it is self-perpetuating and mysteriously autonomous; it "cuts its facets from within./Like jewelry from a grave/it saves itself perpetually and adorns; only itself. . . ." It behooves the soul because it is *like* the soul, not because it is created by it. Because the iceberg is "self-made from elements least visible," because it is *not* dependent upon human sentiment, it is invulnerable and beautiful, "fleshed, fair, erected indivisible."

So it is that in her poems, every one of which *is* a work of art, Elizabeth Bishop stands apart from life at the very moment she engages with it. In this respect her attitude is "Classical" as opposed to "Romantic." As André Gide once said of the classical author, one must look for her "au delà de ses paroles" (on the other side or beyond her words.) Yet all of Miss Bishop's poems have a great deal to do with life. What they express is a way of looking at it. They present us with an interpretation which is at once a simplification and a rough approximation of the world she sees around her; but the interpretation has life and meaning as perhaps the "true" world ultimately never can.

CHAPTER 3

Precision and Resonance

ELIZABETH BISHOP is not an Imagist, but her poetry owes much to those poets who have developed in America the ideas of Imagism into a particular strain of modern poetry. In their different ways, Marianne Moore, William Carlos Williams, Wallace Stevens, and Elizabeth Bishop (and this list is in no way exclusive) have inherited the Imagists' preoccupation with the physical world—their intense concern for what T. E. Hulme called "the earthly and definite." But the poet who was perhaps most responsible for the earthiness of these poets, who did more than anyone to bring "things" back into poetry and who insisted that it be direct, austere, and "free from emotional slither" was undoubtedly Ezra Pound.

Pound was an exception among the Imagists—with whom, indeed, he soon parted company—in that he recognized the value of tradition in poetry while he rejected the limitations of convention. He believed that form should be a function of content, that "some poems may have form as a tree has form, some as water poured into a vase." He emphasized the indispensable virtue of discipline; but he saw clearly that a "vast number of subjects cannot be precisely, and therefore not properly rendered in symmetrical forms." Above all, he opposed easy, sloppy poetry. "The mastery of any art is the work of a lifetime," he wrote; and he practiced the discipline he preached.[1]

Elizabeth Bishop's debt to Pound and to his kind of Imagism is as great as that of any poet of her generation. Stylistically, she profited from his example and learned to write in form without depending upon it—and without abandoning her own intuitive sense of rhythm. Her diction is spare, her ear sure, her standards of craftsmanship high. Like Pound, she has borrowed from many sources. As a girl she was passionately fond of Whitman and later of Hopkins. She admires Baudelaire, Rimbaud, Laforgue, Apollinaire, and Lorca among modern Europeans; but her delight in paradox has given her a special affection for the English lyricists of the sixteenth and seventeenth centuries. Her Baptist upbringing in Nova Scotia taught her the virtue of simple hymns. She has tried her hand at writing in most of these styles and has developed her own voice out of them. She is, in short, a master of her craft.

This mastery would be of very little account, however, if Miss Bishop were not exceptionally gifted in other ways. We have seen that the distinctiveness of her poetry is, at least in part, due to the accuracy of her perceptions. Her images tend to be clear pictures, not abstract impressions. More than this, they have the peculiar force that Pound spoke of when he said that an image should not be a *state* but a *process* of cognition. What Pound meant by image, as Hugh Kenner suggests in his interesting study of Pound, related closely to what Eliot later defined as the "objective correlative." To express emotion, the poet must find a "set of objects, a situation, a chain of events which shall be the formula of that particular emotion; such that when the external facts, which must terminate in sensory experience, are given the emotion is immediately evoked."[2]

If poetic images are "formulae of emotion," they are not simply pictures of objects but pictures of objective things in the process of becoming subjective things. Every object in the flux of life, every event, every "thing" is only known insofar as it is perceived. An Imagist poem, said Pound, "is a poem in which one is trying to record the precise instant when a thing outward and objective transforms itself or darts into a thing inward and subjective."[3] His own one-image poem, "In a Station in the Metro," is a form of what he called "superposition"; it is the setting of one idea on top of another so that this darting process can freely occur: "The apparition of these faces in the crowd;/Petals on a wet, black bough."

Pound's doctrine of the Image is really a way of saying that images in poetry are interpretations as well as imitations. When he spoke of superimposed images, he did not only refer to their juxtaposition on the page. He was suggesting that each image was superimposed upon another or upon others *in the poet's mind.* The feelings—complex and inexplicable—which were evoked by the faces in the Metro station were like the feelings evoked by the petals on the bough. As to *why,* there can be no real explanation. The images in this poem, as Baudelaire might have put it, *correspond* to one another. In the poet's mind they connect with a state of human sensibility.

Images in all good poetry in some way make such a connection. In Western poetry, tropes or figures of speech have generally been used to connect emotions and things by comparing them. Metaphors and their variations (similes, personification, synecdoche, etc.) are customarily made up of two parts. There is a principal subject or what I. A. Richards has called the "tenor" of a metaphor, and there are secondary subjects (Richards calls them "vehicles") which illustrate or amplify the meaning of the principal subject.[4]

Often, but not always, in traditional poetry, the tenor is an abstract idea: life or love or time. In Sir Philip Sidney's line, "Get hence foule Griefe, the canker of the mind," *Griefe,* the abstract concept, is the tenor; and *canker,* the concrete image, is the vehicle. *Canker* gives *Griefe* a specific quality; it makes grief disgusting and undesirable; and the image is the expression of the poet's feelings about both grief and cankers. Again in *Macbeth,* when Macbeth exclaims, "Out, out, brief candle!" Shakespeare gives the abstract idea of life (understood in the context) the concrete qualities of a candle flame. The correspondences between a flame and life are multiple: they are both warm, dangerous, cherished, perilous, beautiful, brief, and so forth.

Modern poets would not quarrel with Shakespeare's and

Sidney's images, but they have tended to agree that, by the end of the nineteenth century, this abstract-concrete type of metaphor, in English poetry at least, was worn out. The Imagists and others, Pound particularly, were plagued by metaphors which were not structural but rhetorical or decorative. They distrusted poetry in which abstract ideas were inappropriately exemplified by trite similes and by inaccurately observed natural phenomena. So they completely turned away from abstract formulations to focus their attention on what was concrete. With the Imagist movement, modern poetry became a poetry of vehicles. *The tenor tended not to be stated.*

Although for anyone familiar with modern poetry this is so obvious a fact that it need only be mentioned in passing, for the reader who knows nothing or little of it such a generalization, oversimplified as it is, may be helpful. What is held to be obscure about modern poetry is not its ideas or, in most cases, its allusions (these can always be explained in footnotes) but its apparent lack of a fixed subject.

Eliot's *The Waste Land,* for instance, is an elaborate and extensive metaphor in which the tenor is implied by the images. It might be added that *The Waste Land* is the more impressive because of this; the reader gets the sense of the poem without confining himself to any one abstract meaning. To explain *The Waste Land*—to say that it is about our lives, about the desolation of civilization, about the horrors of anonymity—is to undervalue its emotional subtlety. No paraphrase can do more than crudely indicate what a good poem is really about, and in the case of *The Waste Land,* the poet has himself refrained from suggesting that there should be a unique interpretation. Eliot leaves his metaphor, so to speak, open at one end. He gives it multiple applicability.

I

Miss Bishop's poems are for the most part modern in the sense that *The Waste Land* is modern, but they are not so complex. Their subjects, or tenors, tend to be implicit and expressed through images. In "Jerónimo's House" the relationship between man's fragile, artificial world and the real one of nature and time is suggested by two simple images: "fairy palace" at the beginning and "hurricane" at the end. The pathos and absurdity and, at the same time, the hopeful dignity of the poem is brought about merely by these references. In the same way, "The Monument," "The Imaginary Iceberg" and "The Map" are images which are symbolic because they are not explained. These are tantalizing and perhaps exasperating poems unless a reader knows that he cannot expect to be able to solve their metaphors exactly in the way he would expect to solve a mathematical equation.

It should be understood that what has been said of images in contemporary poetry does not apply to it alone. Nor is the tenor-vehicle distinction anything more than a crude endeavor to systematize and explain intellectually effects which, for both poet and reader, should be unconsciously felt. It will be plain, too, to anyone who has read much of Elizabeth Bishop's poetry, that she often uses straightforward, classical metaphor. The short poem entitled "The Colder the Air," for instance, is simply a conceit. The poet is amused to observe that a familiar cliché, "piercing cold," can be brought to life. If the cold pierces like arrows, then the atmosphere can be likened to a huntress who shoots the arrows. Her aim is invariably perfect, but not after all so admirable as it seems since "everywhere/her aim is sure, her shot is right/the least of us could do the same." The image is original, but it illustrates a specific concept—the cold.

"From the Country to the City" is another case in point:

> The long, long legs,
> league boots of land, that carry the city nowhere,
>   nowhere; the lines
> that we drive on (satin-stripes on harlequin's
>   trousers, tights):
> his tough trunk dressed in tatters, scribbled over with
>   nonsensical signs. . . .

Obviously the highways out of the city are being compared to the legs of a giant clown. The humor of the last two lines reinforces the conceit with a wry plea: "We bring a message from the long black length of body:/'Subside,' it begs and begs."

It is interesting to compare this straightforward conceit with another poem which is also about New York but in which the city, the tenor in this instance, is not expressed. "The Man-Moth," a title originally suggested by a newspaper misprint for mammoth, is an extended image, a descriptive vehicle in which the feelings of horror, pity, amazement, and disgust that the poet associates with living in the city are evoked not by a description of the city itself but by a description of an equivalent symbol:

> Here, above,
> cracks in the buildings are filled with battered moonlight.
> The whole shadow of Man is only as big as his hat.
> It lies at his feet like a circle for a doll to stand on,
> and he makes an inverted pin, the point magnetized to the moon.
> He does not see the moon; he observes only her vast properties,
> feeling the queer light on his hands, neither warm nor cold,
> of a temperature impossible to record in thermometers.
>
> But when the Man-Moth
> pays his rare, although occasional, visits to the surface,
> the moon looks rather different to him. He emerges
> from an opening under the edge of one of the sidewalks
> and nervously begins to scale the faces of the buildings.
> He thinks the moon is a small hole at the top of the sky,
> proving the sky quite useless for protection.
> He trembles, but must investigate as high as he can climb.
>
> Up the facades,
> his shadow dragging like a photographer's cloth behind him,
> he climbs fearfully, thinking that this time he will manage
> to push his small head through that round clean opening
> and be forced through, as from a tube, in black scrolls on the
> light.
> (Man, standing below him, has no such illusions.)
> But what the Man-Moth fears most he must do, although
> he fails, of course, and falls back scared but quite unhurt.

Then he returns
to the pale subways of cement he calls home. He flits,
he flutters, and cannot get aboard the silent trains
fast enough to suit him. The doors close swiftly.
The Man-Moth always seats himself facing the wrong way
and the train starts at once at its full, terrible speed,
without a shift in gears or a gradation of any sort.
He cannot tell the rate at which he travels backwards.

Each night he must
be carried through artificial tunnels and dream recurrent dreams.
Just as the ties recur beneath his train, these underlie
his rushing brain. He does not dare look out the window,
for the third rail, the unbroken draught of poison,
runs there beside him. He regards it as a disease
he has inherited the susceptibility to. He has to keep
his hands in his pockets, as others must wear mufflers.

If you catch him,
hold up a flashlight to his eye. It's all dark pupil,
an entire night itself, whose haired horizon tightens
as he stares back, and closes up the eye. Then from the lids
one tear, his only possession, like the bee's sting, slips.
Slyly he palms it, and if you're not paying attention
he'll swallow it. However, if you watch, he'll hand it over,
cool as from underground springs and pure enough to drink.

The images in "The Man-Moth" are, on one level, metaphorical in a traditional sense. They are juxtaposed so that one illustrates another: "his shadow dragging like a photographer's cloth," for instance, is straight simile. Perhaps the finest line in the poem is the simile near the end: "one tear, his only possession, like the bee's sting, slips." But these figures of speech are incomplete as they stand. The objects of comparison connect with each other but they resemble a third, unstated something; and this unstated something is the poem's subject.

"The Man-Moth" does not leave quite so much leeway for interpretation as "The Monument." The comparison is between man whose shadow "is only as big as his hat"—who is diminished by the city—and the Man-Moth who, dehumanized and insect-

like, can survive by virtue of his dehumanization. Even for someone who does not know New York, "The Man-Moth" evokes the
mood of a city's personality but is not really an indictment of it.
The Man-Moth is not entirely horrible; rather, he is a pathetic
creature. His loneliness is excruciating; he responds to attention.
He even will give away his life for love. For the significance
of the bee-sting—his only possession—is more than just another
nature image. When the Man-Moth shows his emotion, he must,
like the bee after losing its sting, die.

It is possible to say this much about what "The Man-Moth"
means because, for all its images, it is not Imagist. The Man-
Moth is not a spontaneous, inexplicable image or symbol, as
he in fact might be if the poem were more fragmentary. If the
poem were reduced to a single image, it might read as follows:

> When the Man-Moth
> pays his rare
> although occasional
> visits to the earth's surface,
> he thinks the moon
> is a small hole
> at the top of the sky
> proving the sky
> quite useless for protection.

Probably no reputable Imagist would have written a poem
quite as anchorless as this reduction, but it is interesting to
see what happens to this particular image—an original and impressive one as it stands in the poem—when it is detached from
its context. It is obvious that in my poem the Man-Moth has
lost his specificity. In a short Imagist poem the images cannot
be more than impressions unless, of course, they are explained
by the title or in the poem itself. In a longer poem the poet can,
by the careful juxtaposition and weighting of images, control
their meaning. In "The Man-Moth" Elizabeth Bishop does not
state her tenor, but she so adjusts her vehicles that they apply
to a limited range of experience. The images can be said to be

structural; they present a more or less determined point of view.

Elizabeth Bishop's poems are built, therefore, out of images, but these images are usually interpreted or presented in a way that is consistent with a distinct vision. She is a modern poet in that she often does not state the subjects of her poems but assumes of her readers an awareness and a sensibility which are in tune with her own. Yet she is traditional too, for she usually has something to say which, as far as poetry can conform to ordinary modes of thought, is rational.

II

It will be helpful here to introduce two terms which are relevant to poetry in general but which are particularly relevant to poetry like Elizabeth Bishop's. In all poetry which is essentially inexplicit—which depends upon images and the mental associations of images—a tension must be maintained between the *precision* of the image and the *resonance* of the associations. That is to say, the objective situation must be clear, accurate, and true; but the subjective reaction of the poet (and the reader) must be multiple and complex.

When a poet chooses to express feelings through images, he (or she) chooses to write metaphorically. He chooses to draw on the associations we usually make between sense impressions and emotional responses. Even if a poem is no more than a simple evocation of mood, even if it has no "deeper meaning," the poet is always using *words* with all their overtones of sound and sense to stand for *things* which are perceived by the inarticulate eye or nose or hand. A poet's sense impressions are perhaps sharper than other people's, but they are not different. A poet merely has the ability to select words and patterns of words which suggest accurate connections.

But these connections must be utterly accurate. The poet's words must immediately evoke the reader's experience on one level at least without creating any question of interpretation.

Most good poets have been precise by instinct. Keats's "Ode to Autumn" for instance:

> Then in a wailful choir, the small gnats mourn
> Among the river sallows, borne aloft
> Or sinking as the light wind lives or dies. . . .

A slightly less successful example is Tennyson's "The Eagle":

> He clasps the crag with crooked hands;
> Close to the sun in lonely lands,
> Ringed with the azure world, he stands.
>
> The wrinkled sea beneath him crawls;
> He watches from his mountain walls,
> And like a thunderbolt he falls.

This poem is of special interest because it illustrates how very difficult it is to achieve this quality of precision. "The Eagle" is precise, but it is not quite precise enough. There is, in the first place, the matter of perspective. If the poet is close enough to observe the eagle's crooked hands, then he is in no position to watch it from a distance as it falls "like a thunderbolt." And does an eagle ever fall like a thunderbolt? Because of this failure of precision, the image of the eagle seems to be more imagined than observed. The eagle is endowed with human qualities (hands, moral dignity perhaps) but it has lost its eagle qualities. The image of the sea is better. "The wrinkled sea beneath him crawls" conveys the sense of an alive sea—a sense one often has when looking at it—but the image is true to its actual appearance too.

Resonance is a term which relates closely to its musical origin. One speaks of resonance in poetry as one speaks of overtones in music, but the term here is used metaphorically and with reference to psychological and not physical phenomena.[5] Images in poetry have resonance in the sense that they have multiple meanings. In the psychologists's terminology, they are "over-determined." Resonant images tend also to be symbols.

We have seen that Pound, in his explanation of his "In a Station in the Metro" suggested that an effective image must be both objective and subjective. An objective fact—faces in the crowd—is in this poem "superimposed" on a subjective feeling— the emotional reaction of the poet which somehow associates the faces with petals on a wet, black bough. The resonance of this poem may be said to derive from the tension between the two images: one of them is objective; the other, subjective. We notice that, outside of the association of the images, Pound's poem is ambiguous. We do not know if the emotion is a pleasurable one or if it is unpleasant. Pound, in his commentary, remarks that the faces seemed beautiful to him; the petals on the bough were, for him, images or symbols of something beautiful.[6] It is quite possible, however, to interpret the poem differently. The faces may be pale, ugly, distorted, and wearily alienated from life and for this reason be similar to the dead, withered petals which, on a dreary day in May, lie scattered on the wet boughs of the fruit trees. The images in the poem could support either interpretation because they are not emotively qualified.

"In a Station in a Metro" will serve as an example of the difficulties of maintaining a point of view in Imagist poetry without giving up its enormous possibilities for achieving resonance through ambiguity. Elizabeth Bishop, when she does not write at length, tends to sacrifice clarity of viewpoint—as did the Imagists themselves—in the interests of attempted resonance. In her longer poems she avoids obscurity by relating different images in such a way that a tension between precision and resonance is constantly maintained. The resonance of a poem like "The Monument" is entirely due to what we have spoken of as the multiple applicability of the image. It is precise, and also ambiguous. In shorter, more condensed poems like the following, there is less precision and consequently a failure of resonance. Because the connection between images is unclear, the poem is obscure.

RAIN TOWARDS MORNING

The great light cage has broken up in the air,
freeing, I think, about a million birds
whose wild ascending shadows will not be back
and all the wires come falling down.
No cage, no frightening birds; the rain
is brightening now. The face is pale
that tried the puzzle of their prison
and solved it with an unexpected kiss,
whose freckled unsuspected hands alit.

We might guess that this is a dream poem and that it was, in fact, experienced. Nevertheless, because its images, at least in the last few lines, seem to be private symbols, its resonance does not quite succeed in moving us (although it must be admitted that the image of the rain, juxtaposed with the image of the broken wires of a bird cage, is splendid).

III

If the danger of sacrificing precision for the sake of ambiguity (or of attempting to achieve resonance through obscurity) is very great for a poet like Elizabeth Bishop, there is a comparable danger at the opposite extreme. A poem which is made up of images may well be precise without being resonant. Tennyson's "The Eagle," although it seems a pity to pick on so innocent a poem, has a very meager resonance. The image is not complete or precise enough to convince us that this eagle is any more of a symbol than we take it to be in the normal course of our lives. We can associate Tennyson's bird with the usual clichés of nobility, grandeur, arrogance, and so forth; but, if we compare this poem with any of Marianne Moore's poems about animals, we can see that it is somewhat thin.

Elizabeth Bishop's poems often contain passages which are precise but not resonant; yet, again because the poems tend to be long, such passages never stand alone. In most cases, as we have seen, they relate to the unstated subjects of the poems. In "The Monument," for instance, there are a number of lines which seem to have no intrinsic resonance at all, which sound a little like the descriptions in a text book on architecture:

> From it four thin, warped poles spring out,
> (slanted like fishing-poles or flag-poles)
> and from them jig-saw work hangs down,
> four lines of vaguely whittled ornament
> over the edges of the boxes
> to the ground.

In the poem "A Cold Spring" the following lines occur; out of context, they seem to be almost without resonance, although very precise:

> Finally a grave green dust
> settled over your big and aimless hills.
> One day, in a chill white blast of sunshine,
> on the side of one a calf was born.
> The mother stopped lowing
> and took a long time eating the after-birth,
> a wretched flag,
> but the calf got up promptly
> and seemed inclined to feel gay.

The resonance Elizabeth Bishop achieves in this poem, as in many others, is, as we have seen, not like Pound's. Images like this one in "A Cold Spring" do not "dart into" each other; they stand side by side in stately independence. The poems may be Imagistic in the sense that the images often relate to unstated subjects or tenors, but they do not always have resonance in themselves. In "A Cold Spring" all the images are conventional; they are forms of metaphor or personification:

> For two weeks or more the trees hesitated;
> the little leaves waited,
> carefully indicating their characteristics. . . .

> Greenish-white dogwood infiltrated the wood,
> each petal burned, apparently, by a cigarette-butt. . . .
>
> . . . .
>
> The infant oak-leaves swung through the sober oak.
> Song sparrows were wound up for the summer
> and, in the maple, the complementary cardinal
> cracked a whip and the sleeper awoke,
> stretching miles of green limbs from the south. . . .
>
> . . . .
>
> The bull frogs are sounding
> slack strings plucked by heavy thumbs.
>
> . . . .
>
> Now, from the thick grass, the fireflies
> begin to rise;
> up, then down, then up again:
> lit on the ascending flight
> drifting simultaneously to the same height
> —exactly like the bubbles in champagne.
>
> . . . .

While none of these images, when taken separately, has more
resonance than can be found in ordinary—if original—figures of
speech, taken together in the context of the poem, their very
precision indicates that collectively they have a different sort of
resonance altogether. These images all suggest that a special
relationship is seen by the poet to exist between human and
natural and artificial phenomena. Man and nature imitate each
other; they are seen by the poet as if they could exchange
properties. This point of view—which is the poet's—is itself a
source of resonance; it is not heard but overheard.

What is perhaps most interesting about these images is that
they do not stress the special relevance nature has for man.
Miss Bishop does not see in nature a parable of her own condition; rather, she tends to regard man as part of a continuum
in which everything has, in a very absolute sense, equality. The
poet's joy in spring is the joy of belonging to it, not of elevating

her spirit through it. The mood of "A Cold Spring"—also a resonance—is not therefore ecstatic; it is one of observation, of acceptance, of understanding.

We notice that nothing about the images is *said* in the poem. The poet's presence as interpreter is indispensable, but it appears to be incidental. It is she who is pointing; it is we who are seeing what she points to. The conclusions we arrive at are our own, but they are determined by the poet's way of looking. Again, in "Cape Breton" what appears to be straight description is suddenly given resonance by a subtle intrusion of the poet's interpretive presence:

> Out on the high "bird islands", Ciboux and Hertford,
> the razorbill auks and the silly-looking puffins all stand
> with their backs to the mainland
> in solemn, uneven lines along the cliff's brown grass-frayed edge,
> while the few sheep pastured there go "Baaa, baaa."
> (Sometimes, frightened by aeroplanes, they stampede
> and fall over into the sea or onto the rocks.)

Yet the flatness (and the precision) of these opening lines is deceptive. Without warning, the poem deepens:

> The silken water is weaving and weaving,
> disappearing under the mist equally in all directions,
> lifted and penetrated now and then
> by one shag's dripping serpent neck,
> and somewhere the mist incorporates the pulse,
> rapid but unurgent, of a motorboat.

The notion of "silken water" introduces an element of metaphor which is taken up again with the "shag's dripping serpent neck" (a shag is a kind of cormorant) and further intensified by the implied personification of the motorboat. "The pulse,/rapid but unurgent" not only suggests a human counterpart, but it brings the poet into the poem. It is not the sound of the motor itself that is unurgent, but the sound as it appears to the poet.

Another source of resonance appears about midway through the poem. The stanza begins in the present, prose-like and precise:

> The wild road clambers along the brink of the coast.
> On it stand occasional small yellow bulldozers,
> But without their drivers because today is Sunday.

Then, quite unexpectedly, it expands into a time dimension: "The little white churches have been dropped into the matted hills/like lost quartz arrowheads." There the resonance seems to be due, almost paradoxically, to sheer precision of observation; but the image also has resonance with respect to the whole poem. There is not only a physical resemblance between the churches and the arrowheads but also a historical one. The arrowheads (often found in the hills of North America) and the churches both seem to belong to another age. Beautiful, remote, a little forlorn, they are emblems of the past, of its savagery or of its piety. And with this image the poem takes on new meaning. No longer is it a collage of disparate impressions. It begins to cohere. The images are seen to relate to each other and to the larger theme or idea of the poem itself. For now we see that "Cape Breton" is not only about a place but also about the poet's sense of a place; and this sense has something to do with her feeling for the past and the relationship the past bears to the present.

As if to emphasize this relationship, the matter-of-fact prose style alternates with eloquent, almost rhetorical passages of poetry. The passage which follows is exceptionally, even surprisingly, beautiful. The rhythmic sway of the lines, the half-personification of the road, the sudden rhyming of "see" and "be," the reference to the "admirable scriptures made on stone by stone" (echoing the image of the churches and arrowheads), the surprising synaesthesia of sound and sight at the end—these elements give these lines a resonance which patently would not be so great if they had not been preceded by the prose-like candor of the beginning:

> The road appears to have been abandoned.
> Whatever the landscape had of meaning appears to have been
> abandoned,
> unless the road is holding it back, in the interior,
> where we cannot see,
> where the deep lakes are reputed to be,
> and disused trails and mountains of rock
> and miles of burnt forests standing in grey scratches
> like the admirable scriptures made on stones by stones—
> and these regions now have little to say for themselves
> except in thousands of light song-sparrow songs floating upward
> freely, dispassionately, through the mist and meshing
> in brown-wet, fine, torn fish-nets.

But after this outburst, which is as absolutely precise as it is also resonant, we are tugged back into the civilized world of the present where

> A small bus comes along, in up-and-down rushes,
> packed with people, even to its step,
> (On weekdays with groceries, spare automobile parts, and pump
> parts,
> but today only two preachers extra, one carrying his frock coat
> on a hanger.)
>
> It passes the closed roadside stand, the closed school-house,
> where today no flag is flying
> from the rough-adzed pole topped with a white china door-knob.
>
> It stops, and a man carrying a baby gets off,
> climbs over a stile, and goes down through a small steep meadow,
> which establishes its poverty in a snowfall of daisies,
> to his invisible house beside the water.
>
> The birds keep on singing, a calf bawls, the bus starts.
> The thin mist follows
> the white mutation of its dream;
> an ancient chill is rippling the dark brooks.

At the end of the poem there is a reconciliation. The poet has contrived to link present and past by showing that there is continuity between them. The churches are, after all, used; they are preached in by real preachers one of whom carries his frock coat on a hanger. Yet at the same time the normal, everyday things seem dead. The school and the roadside stand are closed; for a single day they are part of the past which surrounds them and to which, eventually, they will entirely belong.

"The Bight" and "At the Fishhouses" are similar in mood and theme. In them are the same leisurely descriptions of sea and coast, the same flat unexcited tone which sometimes mounts into moving cadences of almost-rhetoric. Moreover, the same interpretive personality broods over the ambivalent nature of perceived things, making of them not philosophies but poetry. As in "Cape Breton," the past lies just beneath the surface of the present, here and there showing through like stones beneath a fresco. These obtrusions are almost always sources of resonance. In "The Bight," for instance,

> Some of the little white boats are still piled up
> against each other, or lie on their sides, stove in,
> and not yet salvaged, if they ever will be, from the last bad storm,
> like torn-open unanswered letters.
> The bight is littered with old correspondences.

Like the image of the churches in "Cape Breton," visual precision and symbolic value exactly match. Nostalgia, unmixed with pathos, is created by the simplest simile. Immediately, however, it is abandoned. The emotion, once suggested, is rigorously held in check, and the last lines are matter-of-fact, common-sensical, wry:

> Click, click. Goes the dredge,
> and brings up a dripping jawful of marl.
> All the untidy activity continues,
> awful but cheerful.

Imagism, like Symbolism, fails as a theory of poetry when the tension between precision and resonance breaks down. When Elizabeth Bishop seeks resonance at the expense of precision— or rather, when she tries to describe private experiences in images which have no reference to specific external objects—she tends to be obscure. In most of her poems, however, Miss Bishop has circumvented the dangers of obscurity by writing at length and with sufficient detail to establish a point of view as the subject or tenor (often unstated) of her poems. The resonance she achieves derives in part from the precision of the images themselves—the kind of precision Pound spoke of and which is present in all good metaphor—but even more from the relationship her images bear to her deeper, unstated themes.

CHAPTER *4*

Sources of Resonance:
A View of Nature

POEMS like "The Man-Moth," "Cape Breton," and "The Bight" are moving and immediately accessible as poetry partly because of the balance they maintain between precision and resonance. But, of course, resonance in poetry is much more than a matter of relating precise descriptions and complex emotions. The sources of resonance upon which Elizabeth Bishop draws are, like those of any genuine poet, so multiple as to be indefinable. What used to be thought of as a poet's inward eye and ear (now we are accustomed to more elaborate psychological terminology) are still responsible for much of what a poet sees and hears as right. Lines like these from "At the Fishhouses," for example, have a rhythmical resonance which goes beyond explanation:

> The water seems suspended
> above the rounded gray and blue-gray stones.
> I have seen it over and over, the same sea, the same,
> slightly, indifferently swinging above the stones,
> icily free above the stones.

We can draw attention here to the alliterative effects, to the onomatopoeia of the "s" sounds which imitate the hissing of the sea, to the swaying rhythm, to the repeated words and phrases which so perfectly match the sense of what is being said (the same sea, the same, slightly, indifferently swaying above the stones/icily free above the stones). There is much in this passage which indeed can be technically analyzed and admired; yet we suspect that whatever might be said of it was not in Miss Bishop's conscious mind as she wrote—that the poet was not aware of using alliteration or onomatopoeia or any particular device but that she heard what she wrote with an ear more sensitive than knowledge.

Later, at the end of the poem, this intensity, with its unfathomable resonance, disappears as the image of the sea is made metaphorical and becomes at once less powerful and more self-conscious. Miss Bishop, departing from her usual practice, brings what she sees and hears into the focus of an abstract idea:

> It is like what we imagine knowledge to be:
> dark, salt, clear, moving, utterly free,
> drawn from the cold hard mouth
> of the world, derived from the rocky breasts
> forever, flowing and drawn, and since
> our knowledge is historical, flowing and flown.

Although this final passage is finely wrought and never obvious, it falls short of her previous vision even though the poem, by literary standards, is still remarkably faultless. The rhyme of "free" and "be" and the internal rhyming of "drawn" and "flown" seem natural and unforced. The image of the ceaseless movement is preserved by the rhythmic flowing of the lines. The anatomical metaphor may seem a little contrived, but it is unobstrusive and imaginatively credible. And yet this second passage lacks the resonance of the former one; and the poem at the end, instead of being nearly a great one, becomes merely a well-trained poem by a good poet.

This is not to deny the general excellence of "At the Fishhouses" but to draw attention to the many sources of resonance which are accessible to the poet and not to the critic—nor even to the poet who, after the moment of insight or vision has

passed, must finish the poem critically with due respect for craft
and judgment. In speaking of resonance and of the sources
of resonance in Elizabeth Bishop's poetry, we need to be aware
that many lines have probably been unconsciously, or at least un-
self-consciously, arrived at, and that the best of her poems,
the ones that bear no trace of cleverness or effort, mean more
than can be said of them.

I

Of the many sources of resonance (other than purely technical
ones) which perhaps can be defined and which seem to show
something of the general nature of Elizabeth Bishop's insight,
there are two which establish her poetry as unmistakably contemporary. The first has to do with her frequent recourse to
personification and with the view of the relationship between
man and nature this personification implies. The second, which
is discussed in the next chapter, regards what has already been
referred to as the ambiguity of appearances.

Personification in poetry (Ruskin called its repeated and
stylized use "the pathetic fallacy") is traditionally a metaphorical
device through which a poet attributes to the non-human world
the appearance, thoughts, or emotions of human beings. In the
Western tradition, personification is generally accepted as normal in the language of description; it is a conventional method,
even in our everyday speech, of saying that one thing is like another. Such familiar expressions as "the trees murmur" or "the
water dances" are instances of personification, although these
"sleeping" metaphors are so securely built into our language that
we scarcely notice them.

Apart from commonplace usages, personification in poetry is
a stylistic device (often a very effective one) for expressing
human emotions—in most cases, emotional reactions *about*
nature. Poets tend to use it, as they use every other form of
metaphor, to make images or symbols of what they feel. In
Keats's "Ode to Autumn," for instance, personification, although

distinctly artificial, succeeds unexceptionally in describing not only a general but a very particular impression of autumn. In quite a different tradition, La Fontaine, in his *Fables*, personified animals in order to caricature or parody human society. Both Keats and La Fontaine, however, although they differed as to purpose, were plainly comfortable in accepting the artificiality of the traditions in which they wrote, for they worked unquestioningly within established esthetic conventions.

Modern poets, too, use metaphors and esthetic conventions. Yet many of them also have a commitment to a form of truth which Keats and La Fontaine might have considered to be irrelevant to poetry. A poet like Elizabeth Bishop, who is sensible of every change in the emotional atmosphere in which she lives, cannot honestly write of nature without being aware, consciously or subconsciously, of what nature actually is. She cannot ignore her awareness that any anthropomorphic depiction of nature is ultimately an esthetic manner of speaking: that, although she is free by virtue of imagination to regard nature as a personified representation of ideas or emotions, she must, if she is to touch upon the truth as she sees it, be conscious of the artifice she employs.

II

Elizabeth Bishop (like Wallace Stevens, Robert Frost, the English poet Ted Hughes, and many others) is a poet much concerned with the truth of nature; and her sense of this truth appears as a kind of ironic counterpoint which plays against or under her conventional metaphors of description. "A Cold Spring" is full of whimsical irony. The reader is reminded all the time that the poet knows she is pretending. The tone of the poem absolves her from believing in her personifications so that, like La Fontaine's animals, they are apt and acute descriptions without being falsifications of fact. When she personifies four deer who "practice" leaping over fences, she is, in describing them, obliquely commenting on human behavior. "The in-

fant oak-leaves swung through the sober oak" is pure metaphor;
it invites a comparison of appearances. The same is true of the
song-sparrow "wound up for the summer" (here, by a curious
inversion, depersonified, imagined as inanimate and mechanical),
of the cardinal who "cracks his whip," and indeed of the landscape itself which stretches "miles of green limbs from the south."

These images in "A Cold Spring," although they pertain to nature, seldom have anything to do with it *as* nature. The poem is,
for the most part, made up of metaphors and conceits, ways
of looking at this or at that piece of scenery. At the very end,
however, and occasionally in the body of the poem, the whimsical comparisons are dropped, and the landscape itself shows
through with glowing exactness:

> Now in the evening,
> a new moon comes.
> The hills grow softer. Tufts of long grass show
> where each cow-flop lies.
>
> . . . .
>
> Now, from the thick grass, the fireflies
> begin to rise:
> up, then down, then up again:
> lit on the ascending flight,
> drifting simultaneously to the same height,
> —exactly like the bubbles in champagne.
> —Later on they rise much higher.
> And your shadowy pastures will be able to offer
> these particular glowing tributes
> every evening now throughout the summer.

This mixture of artifice and naturalness, of wit and of profound emotion is a peculiar one; and it is surprising that it
succeeds so well in "A Cold Spring." The end is perhaps weakened
by the weird urbanity of "exactly like the bubbles in cham-
pagne"—a line which interrupts the sensual sweep (very like
the end of Keats's "Ode to Autumn") of the conclusion. But
here again, we sense that the intrusion is deliberate. The poet

wishes to remain human and civilized and urbane, for to identify too closely with nature is to lose what little dignity she has. Elizabeth Bishop writes with an uneasy awareness of her man-made "shelter from the hurricane"; she allows herself plenty of conventional metaphors (the personification at the end of "At the Fishhouses" is another case in point); but always, in observing nature, she seems to be dimly conscious of herself as the "listener" who is "nothing himself" beholding the "nothing that is not there and the nothing that is."[1] And one can imagine her agreeing with, if not actually writing, Wallace Stevens' "Esthetique du Mal":

> How cold the vacancy
> when the phantoms are gone and the shaken realist
> first sees reality. . . .[2]

Elizabeth Bishop, having seen reality, often endeavors in her poetry not to appear to be shaken. When she personifies natural or artificial objects, she tends to reduce them to human proportions so that personification becomes a source of whimsy. "Seascape" is hardly a nature poem at all but is a social satire. The "white herons got up as angels" and the "gothic" mangrove roots along the Florida coast look like a Catholic heaven. But there is a lighthouse; and it, being Calvinist, thinks that "Hell rages below his iron feet" and that "Heaven is not like flying or swimming,/but has something to do with blackness and a strong glare." The implication of the poem—that the religious struggles of the past were (perhaps like our ideological ones today) differences over imaginary truths—is serious enough. But the tone of the poem is ironic; it is wise rather than profound, witty rather than critical.

In "Florida" nature asserts itself more forcefuly. The poem opens gracefully and whimsically with detached, wry descriptions, as in "A Cold Spring." As in Wallace Stevens' "O Florida, Venereal Soil," the state is personified, depicted as a woman; but Elizabeth Bishop's Indian Princess is not Stevens' "Donna,

donna, dark,/stooping in indigo gown . . ."³ but a less sensual, less personal woman who possesses the attributes of death, not of life:

> The tropical rain comes down
> to freshen the tide-looped strings of fading shells:
> Job's Tear, the Chinese Alphabet, the scarce Junonia,
> parti-colored pectins and Ladies' Ears,
> arranged as on a gray rag of rotted calico,
> the buried Indian Princess's skirt. . . .

In the beginning, the poem, embroidered with metaphors and personifications, is urbane and amusing, almost clinical in its exactness:

> The state with the prettiest name,
> the state that floats in brackish water,
> held together by mangrove roots
> that bear while living oysters in clusters,
> and when dead strew white swamps with skeletons,
> dotted as if bombarded, with green hummocks
> like ancient cannon-balls sprouting grass.
> The state full of long S-shaped birds, blue and white,
> and unseen hysterical birds who rush up the scale
> every time in a tantrum.
> Tanagers embarrassed by their flashiness,
> and pelicans whose delight it is to clown;
> who coast for fun on the strong tidal currents
> in and out among the mangrove islands
> and stand on the sand-bars drying their damp gold wings
> on sun-lit evenings.

But as the poem progresses we begin to feel that, even as the poet personifies and gently mocks the landscape, the landscape in an implicit fashion is passing a judgment on the poet. As in "The Fish," man looking into nature finds there images of his own mind; but nature doesn't return the compliment. Nature does not look back. Its "eyes," like the eyes of the fish are "more like the tipping/of an object toward the light."

Therefore, in spite of its detached, witty tone, "Florida" is a terrifying poem. It is as terrifying as the landscape itself, not because the coastline and swamps are evil in themselves but because, morally, they are nothing at all. They are oblivious of the man's notions of ugliness and beauty, of good and evil. The poet alone cares about such things:

> After dark, the fire-flies map the heavens in the marsh
> until the moon rises.
> Cold white, not bright, the moonlight is coarse-meshed,
> and the careless, corrupt state is all black specks
> too far apart, and ugly whites; the poorest
> post-card of itself.
> After dark, the pools seem to have slipped away.
> The alligator, who has five distinct calls:
> friendliness, love, mating, war, and a warning,
> whimpers and speaks in the throat
> of the Indian Princess.

III

The feeling of barrenness and terror hidden beneath the ornamental façade of "Florida" is the more obvious if the poem is contrasted with some of the nature poems of Marianne Moore, who, for all her biological exactness, ends most of her poems on a note of stoic morality; for instance, the conclusion of Miss Moore's "Virginia Britannia":

> The live oak's darkening filigree
> of undulating boughs, the etched
> solidity of a cypress indivisible
> from the now aged English hackberry,
> become with lost identity,
> part of the ground, as sunset flames increasingly
> against the leaf-chiseled
> blackening ridge of green; while clouds, expanding above
> the town's assertiveness, dwarf it, dwarf arrogance
> that can misunderstand
> importance; and
> are to the child an intimation of what glory is.[4]

In these lines man is dwarfed by a nature in which he is ultimately (as in Wordworth's Immortality Ode) justified. Nature works against the evils of arrogance and self-importance but does so with the goodness and simplicity of childhood. Elizabeth Bishop would probably agree that this is the way things *ought* to be. Yet in her poem man is dissolved in nature altogether. It is as if the personification were also an identification. In the end (in death), man and nature are the same.

This suggestion is perhaps more apparent in another poem about Florida entitled "Little Exercise" in which the positions of man and nature are ironically reversed. The storm rages abroad as if it were alive while the man, as if dead, sleeps:

> Think of the storm roaming the sky uneasily
> like a dog looking for a place to sleep in,
> listen to it growling.
>
> Think how they must look now, the mangrove keys
> lying out there unresponsive to the lightning
> in dark coarse-fibred families,
>
> where occasionally a heron may undo his head,
> shake up his feathers, make an uncertain comment
> when the surrounding water shines.
>
> Think of the boulevard and the little palm trees
> all stuck in rows, suddenly revealed
> as fistfuls of limp fish-skeletons.
>
> It is raining there. The boulevard
> and its broken sidewalks with weeds in every crack,
> are relieved to be wet, the sea to be freshened.
>
> Now the storm goes away again in a series
> of small, badly lit battle-scenes,
> each in "Another part of the field."
>
> Think of someone sleeping in the bottom of a row-boat
> tied to a mangrove root of the pile of a bridge;
> think of him as uninjured, barely disturbed.

Because the storm is seen as an animate, self-perpetuating occurrence which has nothing to do with the man asleep—it neither harms him nor helps him—it reduces him to the level of material objects. The man is a passive participant in nature, the poem suggests; once he is asleep (or dead), he loses, with his personality, his sense of purpose. The only way in which he can raise himself above his environment (and here Elizabeth Bishop comes very close to Wallace Stevens) is through his imagination. In Miss Bishop's poem called "Roosters," the power of imagination and art is seen as the "inescapable hope, the pivot"—as the way in which the things in nature may "come to mean forgiveness." (The next chapter contains a fuller discussion of this poem.)

IV

"Roosters" and "The Fish" are Elizabeth Bishop's most triumphant poems; they are less whimsical, simpler, and more generous than any of her others. We feel in reading them that her uncertainty, her scepticism, and her protective wit have given way to a completely honest realization of what she can accept as both true and good in the world. When she lets the fish go, she does so on purpose; she consciously sees the fish as a symbol of human qualities she admires: courage, beauty, strength, perserverance. And yet she does not personify the fish so we never feel that it is the fish itself who enjoys these attributes. It is she, the poet, who sees *in the real existence of the fish* something which helps her to achieve a moral triumph of her own:

> I stared and stared
> and victory filled up
> the little rented boat,
> from the pool of bilge
> where oil had spread a rainbow
> around the rusted engine
> to the bailer rusted orange,
> the sun-cracked thwarts,
> the oarlocks on their strings,
> the gunnels—until everything
> was rainbow, rainbow, rainbow!
> And I let the fish go.

As has already been suggested, it is difficult to attribute a specific philosophy of nature to Elizabeth Bishop other than that which appears implicitly in her poems. Unlike Wallace Stevens, whom she in so many ways resembles, she has never claimed to have a philosophy. Indeed, her perceptions are the better for not being held to the measure of abstract ideas. She is not a true sceptic, for life has immense meaning and value for her. Nor is she, in spite of her sense of the ultimate unity of things, a mystic. Her prevailing secularism and her sharp common sense prevent her revelations from being anything more than temporary insights.

Perhaps the best that can be said of her "philosophy" is that it is not a philosophy at all but a remarkable instinctive awareness. Her poetry implies that there is an inscrutable equality among all human and natural things and that they are subject to the same ruthless, mysterious forces. At the same time, she sees man as a conscious being, capable of understanding, or of at least feeling, something of these forces. His life is meaningful as his eye (and his mind's eye) sees and as his imagination interprets. Without vision or understanding, however, he is wholly absorbed into the universe which, after he is gone, continues: "La vie humaine continue/Sans toi, defunte devenue."[5] These lines of Jules Laforgue find an echo in Elizabeth Bishop's "Cootchie." Cootchie, once Miss Lula's servant, now "lies in marl . . . below the surface of the coral-reef" forever unaware of the world which she never, in fact, "knew":

> Cootchie, Miss Lula's servant, lies in marl,
> black into white she went
>   below the surface of the coral-reef.
> Her life was spent
>   in caring for Miss Lula, who is deaf,
> eating her dinner off the kitchen sink
> while Lula ate hers off the kitchen table.
> The skies were egg-white for the funeral
>   and the faces sable.

Tonight the moonlight will alleviate
the melting of the pink wax roses
    planted in tin cans filled with sand
placed in a line to mark Miss Lula's losses;
    but who will shout and make her understand?
Searching the land and sea for someone else
    the lighthouse will discover Cootchie's grave
and dismiss all as trivial; the sea, desperate,
    will proffer wave after wave.

CHAPTER 5

The Ambiguity of Appearances

W E HAVE SEEN in Chapter II that many of Elizabeth Bishop's poems are essentially verbal pictures—pictures not only of things, places, and people but of her way of looking at things, places, and people. The poems are images of interpretations. But we have also noted that Miss Bishop frequently gives resonance to her poems by suggesting that, within or beyond the images she shows us, there are possibly many interpretations, although these may be relative to specific objects. In other words, there seems to be a discrepancy in her poetry between what can be seen and what can be known—between the surfaces of things which are observed and the significance or meanings of these surfaces which, for Elizabeth Bishop, are in their very nature ambiguous.

This characteristic is particularly evident in a poem like "Faustina or Rock Roses" in which the problem of interpretation—in this case, the interpretation of the facial expression of an old, black servant—is specifically raised. "Faustina" is both like a picture and like looking at a picture. The picture is a portrait; two women, one black and one white, are arranged against a background of contrasting shades of white. The frail, dying white woman on the bed of "chipped enamel" which blooms above her head "into four vaguely rose-like/flower formations" is "betrayed" along with the visitor and the room by a naked eighty-watt bulb which hangs from the ceiling:

It exposes the fine white hair,
the gown with the undershirt
showing at the neck,
the pallid palm-leaf fan
she holds but cannot wield
her white disordered sheets
        like wilted roses.

Clutter of trophies,
chamber of bleached flags!
——Rags or ragged garments
hung on the chairs and hooks
each contributing its
shade of white, confusing
        as undazzling.

These visual motifs—the whites and roses—recur and inter-
weave throughout the poem; against them, the black, portentous,
enigmatic figure of the servant Faustina looms sinister and
pathetic:

On bare scraping feet
Faustina nears the bed.
She exhibits the talcum powder,
the pills, the cans of 'cream',
the white bowl of farina,
requesting for herself
        a little *coñac*;

complaining of, explaining,
the terms of her employment.
She bends above the other.
Her sinister kind face
presents a cruel black
coincident conundrum.
        Oh, is it

freedom at last, a lifelong
dream of time and silence,
dream of protection and rest?
Or is it the very worst,
the unimaginable nightmare
that never before dared last
        more than a second?

Faustina's paradoxical expression takes the poem, as it were, out of the picture and into the mind of the poet (the visitor). The visual impression—the confused whites, the rose patterns of the bed, the pattern of the tacks on the wall paper, "violet-embossed, glistening/with mica flakes"—gives rise to an interpretive question. What does Faustina's "sinister kind face" mean? What does she want? What does she really feel?

> The acuteness of the question
> forks instantly and starts
> a snake-tongue flickering;
> blurs further, blunts, softens,
> separates, falls, our problems
> becoming helplessly
> proliferative.

In this stanza Elizabeth Bishop comes as near as she ever does to formulating an abstract idea. In the final stanza, the poem, having reached the limits of interpretive speculation, retreats again into the picture. It withdraws from questions which never can be answered and returns at last—but with an enormous increase in resonance—to tangible surfaces, to visible impressions, which are *all that can be known*:

> There is no way of telling.
> The eyes say only either.
> At last the visitor rises,
> awkwardly proffers her bunch
> of rust-perforated roses
> and wonders oh, whence come
> all the petals.

In painting, and particularly in portrait painting, the question raised in "Faustina" (the question of the meaning of appearances) is a natural concomitant of the art which evokes it. Visible surfaces are all that a painter can ever give us: we can only *infer* from an arrangement of shapes and colors on a canvas what a given painting "says." This is true not only of contemporary art but of painting in any period.[1] Certain portraits of

Rembrandt, for instance, are full of resonant ambiguity for precisely this reason. Is Pilate's expression, as he leans down to wash his hands, one of contempt, of boredom, of stupidity, of deliberate insensitivity, of despairing puzzlement—or a combination of these or other emotions? Again, what meaning can be attributed to the facial expression of the old woman cutting her fingernails? Or from the many self-portraits Rembrandt did of himself? It is the acuteness of *this* kind of question that so often starts the snake tongue flickering in Elizabeth Bishop's mind; and it is significantly the hopelessness of answering it that is a source of her persistent questioning and doubt.

I

For the most part, Elizabeth Bishop's preoccupation with surfaces reflects her painter-like fascination with appearances in themselves. Instinctively, she looks first and thinks later. In this respect she is more like Wallace Stevens (who at one time greatly influenced her) than he sometimes is like himself. That is to say, the minutiae always mean more to her than "clouds, benevolences, distant heads."[2] She lives in richness in the midst of a physical world and, by implication at least, rejects all notions of higher essences—both of God and reason—through which Western man has striven to rise above himself in the past. Like Stevens, too, she is sceptical and stoic, drawn into questioning the possibility of knowing anything absolutely in a world without tangible absolutes.

While Stevens asserts, however, that the things of the world are sufficient and plays word games with his realist metaphysics (*Not Ideas about the Thing but the Thing Itself*), Elizabeth Bishop offers no solutions to questions but the *questions* themselves. So, in contrast to Stevens, who is the supreme atheist, the towering Realist, the self-proclaimed scoffer of God and reason as he is celebrator of surfaces and physical sensations, Elizabeth Bishop is doubtfully and modestly agnostic. If there is any "philosophy" in her work, it is not of a metaphysical

variety; it is an empirical philosophy of particulars. As in "The
Map," questions are often raised and then left hanging, half
comically, without answers: "Along the fine tan sandy shelf/
is the land tugging at the sea from under?"

The question is quizzical (the whole poem verges on the
edge of whimsical personification, and, of course, has no pretensions to being philosophical); yet, that the land might be
seen as lifting the sea from under suggests that the *way* things
are seen affects what in fact *is* seen, that interpretation is always
part of seeing in the sense that it enables us to know what we
see. Stevens suggests the same thing in his "Sea Surface Full
of Clouds." In a series of refrains he provides flamboyant,
metaphorical answers to his speculative question:

> Who, then, evolved the sea-blooms from the clouds
> Diffusing balm in that Pacific calm?
> C'était mon enfant, mon bijou, mon âme. . . .[3]

In Stevens' poetry, philosophical considerations are often given
the status of poetical subjects; or, at least, the answers he af-
firms with so much gusto are to questions which are philosophical by implication. The question of the existence of higher
metaphysical essences is raised by a plethora of gaudy and
encouraging negatives (see, for instance, "Sunday Morning").
Again, only the narrow-mindedness of stereotyped rationalism
could have provoked this derisive jocularity (the image, i.e., the
rationalists in square hats, is borrowed from Pascal):

> Rationalists, wearing square hats,
> Think in square rooms,
> Looking at the floor,
> Looking at the ceiling.
> They confide themselves
> to right angled triangles.
> If they tried rhomboids,
> Cones, waving lines, ellipses—
> As, for example, the ellipse of the half-moon—
> Rationalists would wear sombreros.[4]

Such declarations do much to entertain us. However, as ideas they are more relevant to our personal and social problems ("how can we come to terms with this world?") than to a serious philosophy of nature. Indeed, for all its gaiety and generosity of imagination, Stevens' "philosophy" consists of little more than a set of practical esthetic attitudes which he decorates with bizarre colors in order to shock the grey bulk of humanity into imagination. Compare, for instance, the amusing but relatively complaisant acceptance of face values at the end of his "So and So Reclining on her Couch" with the uneasy "exhilaration" of Elizabeth Bishop's "Gentleman of Shalott." Stevens writes:

> She floats in the contention, the flux
>
> Between the thing as idea and
> the idea as thing. She is half who made her.
> This is the final Projection, C.
>
> The arrangement contains the desire of
> The artist. But one confides in what has no
> Concealed creator. One walks easily
>
> The unpainted shore, accepts the world
> As anything but sculpture. Good-bye,
> Mrs. Pappadopoulos, and thanks.[5]

In contrast, Elizabeth Bishop becomes so preoccupied with the nature of experience and with the complexity of the questions experience provokes that, in the end, she can answer them only provisionally, if at all:

> There's little margin for error,
> but there's no proof, either.
> And if half his head's reflected,
> thought, he thinks, might be affected. . . .

The Gentleman of Shalott is resigned to his "economical design," but Elizabeth Bishop is less easily satisfied. In a short and surprisingly imageless poem entitled "Conversation" she suggests that words themselves are so elusive and inexplicable that even self-communication is impossible:

> The tumult in the heart
> keeps asking questions.
> And then it stops and undertakes to answer
> in the same tone of voice.
> No one would tell the difference.
>
> Uninnocent these conversations start,
> and then engage the senses,
> only half-meaning to.
> And then there is no choice,
> and then there is no sense;
>
> until a name
> and all its connotation are the same.

For Elizabeth Bishop, doubt about the meaning of appearances leads to doubt about the nature of experience itself and inevitably, too, to doubts about the means by which experience can be described or understood. Under her eyes the world (as earlier under Hofmannsthal's; see Chapter II) is perpetually on the point of dissolving into its chaotic, component particles. It coheres; it is *made* to have meaning only as it is seen, as it is created by a human mind. Because Elizabeth Bishop is an artist, she, like Stevens, puts great emphasis on the organizing power of the imagination. The final quatrain of Miss Bishop's poem entitled "Sunday 4 a.m." can be understood as an appeal to the principle of artistic order:

> The world seldom changes,
> but the wet foot dangles
> until a bird arranges
> two notes at right angles.

The mixture of a natural and a geometrical image in this stanza (the bird who arranges two notes at right angles) suggests exactly that impulse Elizabeth Bishop has to be precise in her search for order and beauty in the midst of chaos. Her mind has not Stevens' superabundance of energy. Her particularizing imagination does not easily spill over the boundary of art into metaphysics. There is no radiant diffusion of ideas and images. Nonetheless, within her somewhat narrower range, concentration and penetration coexist in equal proportions; and they limit her areas of concern as a mathematician or a scientist limits his field of investigation. Therefore, although she is less interested in philosophy than Stevens, she tends to be a better "philosopher"; or rather, she tends to raise unconsciously the kind of problems that modern philosophers have raised for different reasons.

II

It should be said from the outset that Elizabeth Bishop, by her own confession, has never studied Wittgenstein's *Philosophical Investigations* and makes no pretension at all to being a philosopher herself. So there is no question of her being influenced. Indeed, if she had been influenced, it is likely that her poetry would have suffered; for, while the problems of poets and philosophers at given times in history are often similar, their *aims* are almost certain to be different. Poets rarely make philosophies, but they record more accurately, perhaps, than do the theorists themselves the effect that philosophical ideas have on human feelings. So it happens that the kind of ambiguity with which Elizabeth Bishop invests her fine perceptions derives from a philosophical notion of reality which is very like Wittgenstein's, even though, in all probability, she has never been conscious of the similarity.

Wittgenstein's *Philosophical Investigations* (first published in England in 1953, although the views there expounded were known to his students at least two decades earlier) are principally concerned with problems of knowing—with that branch of philosophy known as epistemology. How do we know, he asks, what words mean when they refer to sensations? How do we communicate feelings? What is the philosophical concept of meaning in connection with language? How can we describe what we know? Or do we, in fact, ever know whether what we say we know is true or not?

The very fact that Wittgenstein felt unable to coordinate his thoughts (he calls them "remarks") into a systematic philosophy but published them instead as a series of random paragraphs suggests that he shared in large measure the sense of fragmentation and doubt which we have already spoken of in connection with Hofmannsthal. The *Philosophical Investigations*, indeed, are as tortured and fragmentary a document as any major literary work of the twentieth century. It is unfinished —and unfinishable. The introduction suggests that, in pursuit of truth, Wittgenstein could not in conscience force his thoughts into a logical system which, however desirable and convenient, might not be true:

> . . . my thoughts were soon crippled if I tried to force them on in any single direction against their natural inclination.—And this was, of course, connected with the very nature of the investigation. For this compels us to travel over a wide field of thought criss-cross in every direction.—The philosophical remarks in this book are, as it were, a number of sketches of landscapes which were made in the course of these long and involved journeyings.[6]

Wittgenstein's "long and involved journeyings" took place, of course, in the world of ideas; with respect to the questions they raised, however, they were not unlike Elizabeth Bishop's physical voyages. The question of the meaning of appearances, for instance, is continually occurring. How can I ever *know*, Wittgenstein asks himself, whether another man is in pain or not? He may cry out; he may screw up his face in an expression which *looks* like an expression of pain; but do I ever feel his pain? If not, then how can I know that he really is in pain? "If I say of myself that it is only from my own case that I know what the word 'pain' means—must I not say the same of other people too? And how can I generalize the one case so irresponsibly?"[7] Thus, although we seem to know what the word "pain" means, we know, in fact, only a word which we sometimes associate with a private sensation. But we never know generally what the abstract "something" is which we want to signify when we use the word "pain."

Again, the question of the interpretation of appearances arises in connection with pictures:

> I see a picture which represents a smiling face. What do I do if I take the smile now as a kind one, now as malicious? Don't I often imagine it within a spatial and temporal context which is either of kindness or malice? Thus I might supply the picture with the fancy that the smiler was smiling down on a child at play or again at the suffering of an enemy.[8]

> (There is no way of telling.
> The eyes say only either.)

It will be plain even from these brief examples that in the *Philosophical Investigations*, the question of reality—of what lies behind or within appearances—is subject to a scrutiny of a sort never dreamed of by most earlier philosophers. Any Hegelian notion of an ultimate reality or essence which exists *apart* from our sensations and experience seems to be an impossibility; and yet the notion persists that there is *something* which is sensed: "The observer does not produce what is observed!"[9] When we see something, Wittgenstein suggests, we tend to see it "according to an interpretation." A drawing of a triangle, for instance, can be seen as "a triangular hole, as a solid, as a geometrical drawing, as standing on its base, as hinging from its apex, as a mountain, as a wedge, as an arrow, a pointer and as various other things."[10] But *seeing as* is not the same as *seeing*, and the question of what, in fact, seeing is, apart from the *way* we see, remains a heart-ambiguity of his philosophy.

We sense in reading her poetry, that for Elizabeth Bishop, too, the ultimate ambiguity of experience derives not from the non-existence of reality but from the utter impossibility of knowing it. It is not reality which is impossible but an absolute human interpretation of reality. The feeling of frustration, of loss, of having missed something which appears in so many poems (for instance, in "Chemin de Fer," "Faustina," "Sleeping Standing Up") is not defined as it would be in philosophy or psychology, but it is suggested by recurring images of frustrated search:

> How stupidly we steered
> until the night was past
> and never found out where the cottage was.

The poem that ends with these lines is a dream poem ("Sleeping Standing Up"), but the remark might pass for a summary of Elizabeth Bishop's sense of experience in general.

It is worth pointing out that the particular *angst* from which Elizabeth Bishop suffers springs (like Wittgenstein's, perhaps) not from a lack of *moral* certainty—as it does, apparently, in the case of Existentialist writers who seek to interpret human nature in terms of individual moral responsibility—but from a profound sense of human ignorance. Morally, Elizabeth Bishop is as incorruptible and unquestioning as Marianne Moore; Miss Bishop is as humane and sympathetic in her concern for others as she is stoic in her acceptance of life. Practically, she prefers to have her miracle for breakfast:

> My crumb
> my mansion, made for me by a miracle,
> through ages, by insects, birds, and the river
> working the stone. Every day, in the sun,
> at breakfast time I sit on my balcony
> with my feet up, and drink gallons of coffee.

It is the question of the right interpretation of the world, of the uncertain texture of what is known, that continually puzzles and eludes her.

ELIZABETH BISHOP

III

The problem is not one that concerns artists and philosophers alone; indeed, artists, on the whole, have been rather slower than mathematicians and scientists in coming to grips with the question of reality in its fullest sense. The discovery of non-Euclidian geometries took place in the 1820's and 1830's, and the notion of fixed, *a priori* truths in mathematics became untenable. The tendency now is to regard the theorems of mathematics (as indeed, the numbers) as existing *only* in application: there is no "meaning" in mathematics which is united in some mysterious way to the symbols; "instead [meaning] is the application of the symbols and we have command over these."[11] When, then, in 1823, the Hungarian mathematician Janos Bolyai, one of the founders of non-Euclidean geometry, wrote to his father that he had from nothing created another wholly new universe, he was implying that *the way we know* the universe is dependent upon *our* ideas. In effect, all that we know of the universe is man-made.[12]

Again, if mathematical truths can be shown to be "created," how is it possible to have a notion of *a priori* truths in physics? The theory of relativity developed by Einstein, together with Heisenberg's formulation of the indeterminacy principle in quantum mechanics (see note 13, page 133), seems to suggest disturbingly that the proofs of science are also man-made ones capable of fitting empirical observations approximately but not absolutely—that science is indeed a wonderful but provisional method of examining a universe which no one is able perfectly to know. "If there is any absolute truth in physics," writes Dr. David Bohm in the last chapter of a serious consideration of modern physics, "it is relativity itself that is absolute . . . it is stated to be the only absolute truth that there is no absolute content to our knowledge at all."[13]

The world that science has made, then, and in which the twentieth century must believe, is a world without absolutes.

Behind the mists of seeming there are not, as we normally assume, solid mountains of facts but more mists; and, behind these, there are more mists still. Like the inhabitants of Plato's Cave, we live among shadows and apparitions. But the walls of the cave are no more than a magnificent stage set: a series of elaborately painted flats which man is continually creating for himself out of the tireless working of his own mind. To most people, the perilous frailty of the scenery is not apparent, and they live within the compass of experience, content or discontent with what it brings them. But there are a few who are engaged in painting the scenes; and they, as they work, occasionally perceive that the canvas ripples as if an icy wind were blowing behind it. Through the minute cracks in the surface appears not the shining Absolute of Plato, but the *espaces infinies* of Pascal—the void, the orderless, formless, timeless, senseless eternity within which man has somehow constructed for himself a "fairy palace."

It is perhaps understandable in view of the artists' larger commitment to human values that surprisingly few twentieth-century poets have developed as a source of resonance a sense of the true mysteriousness and terror of the scientist's world. Among poets, Robert Frost, oddly conventional in other respects, is a notable exception; his sense of the enormity and incomprehensibility of the unhuman universe contrasts ironically with his colloquial style and gives his poetry a depth which sometimes becomes greatness. Randall Jarrell comments brilliantly on some of Frost's lesser known poems such as "Directive" and "The Most of It" in his essay entitled "To the Laodiceans" (reprinted recently in *Poetry and the Age*).[14]

On the whole, however, and particularly in the visual arts, artists still tend to speak of "reality" as if it had some separate and semi-mythical existence. The Surrealists in the 1920's and 1930's, for instance, made a great stir about the reality of the subconscious. But what is this reality if not simply another way of seeing and apprehending experience? Even Paul Klee, who was among the most sincere and unostentatious of the abstractionists, seems to have believed that there was some sort of ultimate reality which could be revealed through art. "In earlier times," he wrote in the *Schöpferische Konfession* in 1920,

> artists liked to show what was actually visible, either the things they liked to look at or things they would have liked to have seen. Nowadays we are concerned with reality rather than with the merely visible; we therefore express our belief that the visible realm is no more than a "special case" in relation to the cosmos, and that other truths have potentially greater weight. In our pictures, the visible appearances of things have a wider and more complex meaning, which often seems to contradict the rational experience of yesterday. We are striving for the essence that hides behind the fortuitous.[15]

The "essence" expressed in painting—whether we mean the "created space" of the Cubists or the fantastical symbolism of the Surrealists—can be, however, no more real in an ultimate sense than are the biologist's microphotographs of cells or the psychiatrist's analyses of dreams. In other words, it is quite true that both art and science have been affected by the breakdown of theoretical dogma in their respective fields and that, as Klee says, the visible realm is now considered to be no more than "a special case." But whether we can say a reality exists beyond our interpretations of experience is a question which no one can answer.

IV

Elizabeth Bishop is more doubtful, more secular, more pessimistic, and in a certain sense more "modern" than many poets who are objectively "greater" than she is because she is always true to her sense of ignorance. Eliot and Pound, for instance, have had more to say; their command of language and their scope of knowledge are far more impressive. Yet each of them, in the end, needed the support of an artificially resurrected tradition. The unbearable uncertainty of the contemporary world led Eliot back into a conservative religion and Pound into a madhouse. Wallace Stevens shared Miss Bishop's secularism, as well as her painter's passion for color and form; but his obsession with the apparent discrepancy between ideas and things diverted his attentions to philosophy; and, in the end, this concern warred against the clarity of his imaginative perceptiveness. As for Marianne Moore, she is a poet who is, above all, fascinated by the stage set, by the sheer scenery of the world. Her work therefore (and perfectly legitimately) begs philosophical questions altogether. Its resonance derives from its fanatical precision, its exotic angles of vision, its "priceless set of vocabularies," and its resolute denial of despair. This denial is in contrast to Elizabeth Bishop whose poetry, for all its wit and whimsicality, comes from the heart of despair itself.

But despair, for Elizabeth Bishop, is rarely an occasion for romantic despondency or for virulent sarcasm as it sometimes was for her mentors Laforgue and Apollinaire. It is rather an opportunity for elegance. The fineness of form, the wit, the poignant irony of control which are the essence of her art can be found similarly in the music of Anton von Webern. Webern was, like Wittgenstein, unable to force his moments of insight in directions against his natural inclinations. His is a music of remarks, of momentary glimpses of "whatever it is one can never really see full-face but that seems enormously important."[16] Elizabeth Bishop's poems, are by contrast, flowing and more generous; but she shares Webern's unwillingness to pretend. Brevity, uncertainty, ignorance, and terror are accepted as the conditions of a sense of truth—and of beauty.

For Elizabeth Bishop, indeed, beauty is all that can be salvaged from the ambiguity and the chaos of existence. It is a kind of answer, a kind of resolution. However, Elizabeth Bishop's beauty has a very subtle and elusive existence so that she is not always sure that it is beauty at all. Miss Bishop's is not Keats's Truth; hers is not Marianne Moore's beauty which is "everlasting" while "dust is for a time."[17] Hers is not even

Wallace Stevens' beauty of order which is "momentary in the mind" but in the flesh (in memory and imagination) immortal.[18] Human memory and imagination seem rather, for Miss Bishop, to be made of perishable stuff. Like the monument, they are mysterious, indecipherable, and somehow evolving; they are made of wood which has the qualities of both the living and the non-living world:

> . . . Wood holds together better
> than sea or cloud or sand could by itself,
> much better than real sea or sand or cloud
> . . . .
> It may be solid, may be hollow.
> The bones of the artist prince may be inside
> or far away on even dryer soil.
> But roughly but adequately it can shelter
> what is within (which after all
> cannot have been intended to be seen . . .)

We have the sense that, for Elizabeth Bishop, beauty itself is ambiguous (it might, under different circumstances, be ugliness) and that it depends upon or is in some way drawn out of the same ambiguity of appearances which circumscribes all human perception.

In the poem "Roosters," the poet's feeling for the relationship between life and art, and that between life and art and the something else that she means by beauty (that "never can be seen full face"), is suggested with that curious combination of irony and gentleness which gives the best of Miss Bishop's poetry its great distinction. On an obvious level, "Roosters" contrasts the beauty, the synthesis, of art and religion with the horror of "real" life. The raucous cries of the roosters which grate upon the morning "like a wet match" are seen to symbolize the stupidity and uselessness not only of the roosters' lives but of man's. Vain, stupid, and quarrelsome, each one an active/displacement in perspective;/ each screaming, 'This is where I

live,'" the roosters are emblems of a cruel, arrogant humanity.
The poet addresses them scornfully:

> You whom the Greeks elected
> to shoot at on a post, who struggled
> when sacrificed, you whom they labeled
>
> "Very combative" . . .
> what right have you to give
> commands and tell us how to live,
>
> cry "Here!" and "Here!"
> and wake us here where are
> unwanted love, conceit and war?

Later on in the poem, there is war. The scene is a comical,
horrible human parody:

> And one has fallen,
> but still above the town
> his torn-out, bloodied feathers drift down;
>
> and what he sung
> no matter. He is flung
> on the grey ash heap, lies in dung
>
> with his dead wives
> with open, bloody eyes,
> while those metallic feathers oxidize.

But at this point the poem changes course. The roosters are
taken out of their dung-filled barnyard and transferred into the
allegory of Christian art. The rooster's death brings to mind
St. Peter's denial of Christ and conjures up an image of Christian
forgiveness. Human beings, after all, are *not* roosters, for they
are able to conceive of salvation:

> Old holy sculpture
> could set it all together
> in one small scene, past and future:
>
> Christ stands amazed,
> Peter, two fingers raised
> to surprised lips, both as if dazed.

But in between
a little cock is seen
carved on a dim column in the travertine,

explained by *gallus canit;*
flet Petrus underneath it.
There is inescapable hope, the pivot.

Yes, and there Peter's tears
run down our chanticleer's
sides and gem his spurs.

Tear-encrusted thick
as a medieval relic
he waits. Poor Peter, heart-sick,

still cannot guess
those cock-a-doodles yet might bless,
his dreadful rooster come to mean forgiveness,

a new weathervane
on basilica and barn,
that outside the Lateran

there would always be
a bronze cock on a porphyry
pillar so the people and the Pope might see

that even the Prince
of the Apostles long since
had been forgiven, and to convince

all the assembly
that "Deny deny deny,"
is not all the roosters cry.

And so the poem becomes, in the second section, a declaration of hope. For men, roosters have "come to mean forgiveness." There is a possibility of faith, of a better life.

Another poet (one thinks of Marianne Moore) might have ended the poem with this *denial* of despair, with the brave affirmation of "Deny deny deny/ is not all the roosters cry."[19] But Elizabeth Bishop, for whom the synthesis of faith or even of art is never long and never constant, returns in the end to the world, to the physical world which, no longer ugly and sinister, has become beautiful with the rising of the sun:

> In the morning
> a low light is floating
> in the backyard, and gilding
>
> from underneath
> the broccoli, leaf by leaf;
> how could the night have come to grief?
>
> gilding the tiny
> floating swallow's belly
> and lines of pink cloud in the sky,
>
> the day's preamble
> like wandering lines in marble.
> The cocks are now almost inaudible.
>
> The sun climbs in,
> following "to see the end,"
> faithful as enemy, or friend.

The beauty of this homely landscape is so exquisitely described in these lines (notice the repetition of "gilding": the swallow and the broccoli are equally beautiful in sunlight; and where, in any poetry, is there a visual description of a morning sky more lovely and exact than "the day's preamble/like wandering lines in marble"?) that it is easy to miss their full implication. How very neatly they suggest that beauty is, like good and evil, a human creation. The roosters, "now almost inaudible," who have been seen in the course of the poem first as symbols of evil and then as symbols of good, disappear as symbols with the coming of the sun. And under the sun, art and religion are also forgotten. They leave only their afterglow: traces of human hope which are now hardly needed. The sun, "faithful as enemy or friend," is a final symbol of the ambiguity of all symbols. The transient beauty of the morning—unlike art, which is after all only a compensation, only a man-made escape from the man-made evil of the world, forgives nothing, tells us nothing, explains nothing—is simply itself.

CHAPTER 6

A Last Word

FOR A POET whose work will, in all probability, survive after many names and reputations of the twentieth century are forgotten, Elizabeth Bishop has written surprisingly little. Moreover, those poems for which she is famous (*The Fish, Roosters, The Monument*) are not poems of a kind that are, for extra-literary reasons, especially popular today. They do not reveal the bruised spirit of an artist made callous (or mad) by a brutal society. They do not plead for sympathy. They are not pathetic, violent, sentimental, theoretical, or cynical. They are not self-flattering and show no trace of egomania. They are not mystical; they are not even, very often, social criticisms.

Yet I believe that Elizabeth Bishop's poems will survive because they reflect some very personal qualities which are rarely found in conjunction with a creative personality. Elizabeth Bishop is modest, and she is dignified. Because she is modest, she has not presumed to assign to her artistic sensibilities an importance incommensurate with their value. Hers may be a minor voice among the poets of history, but it is scarcely ever a false one. We listen to it as one might listen to a friend whose exceptional wisdom and honesty we gratefully revere.

Because Elizabeth Bishop is dignified she has been reluctant to fling her troubles at the world; she prefers always to see herself with a certain wry detachment. As a result, her poems are occasionally artificial; there is sometimes a coy archness which undermines the strength of her deeper perceptions. On the other hand, her tone savors more good manners than of mannerism. She would not insult us as she tells us the often unflattering truth.

In the age and civilization and country to which we belong—an age of economic extravagance and spiritual bankruptcy; a civilization on the point of extinguishing itself, or of reaching the moon by space ship; a country in which nature is becoming more and more scientifically comprehensible at the same time as it is ignored or polluted or patronized by the multitudes who have reduced miles of America to a hideous waste—it is unquestionably difficult to maintain an attitude of comprehensive detachment. It is easier to hate, to rebel, to escape, to deplore—or even to sentimentalize. Wit and delicacy of feeling do not thrive where there is mass insensitivity, inconceivable ugliness, and devastating "progress."

But, if poetry cannot succeed in maintaining the values of detachment and understanding at the same time that it remains morally committed to the values of personal affection, wisdom and beauty, what can? Many poets of the present century have been driven to despair by the loss of their spiritual and humanist illusions. But if there is to be any poetry in the future, perhaps this poetry will have to be written without such illusions; for can anyone who calls himself poet afford to retreat from the insights of his age?

Elizabeth Bishop is a realist, but she sees miracles all the time. In her poems it is as if she were turning again and again to say to us: "If man, who cannot live by bread alone, is spiritually to survive in the future, he must be made to see that the stuff of bread is also the stuff of the infinite." The crumb which becomes a mansion in "A Miracle for Breakfast' is more than a clever poetical conceit. It is a symbol of hope in a world which can be bearable—for some mysterious reason—in spite of its evils.

A Note on Miss Bishop's Critics

As a result, perhaps, of her own good taste and reticence, Elizabeth Bishop has been spared much of the critical battering which in the past thirty years has been so liberally dispensed by our literary journals. She has always had, however, a devoted following of poets in America, while some of the most intelligent criticism of her work has come out of England.

As early as 1935 Ann Winslow published a selection of Elizabeth Bishop's poems (including "The Map") in an anthology entitled *Trial Balances* (New York, 1935). To this selection Marianne Moore appended some brilliant, oblique comments which draw attention to the "rational considering quality" of Miss Bishop's work and to its originality. Miss Moore has also written perceptively of *The Diary of 'Helena Morley'*; her remarks about Miss Bishop's translation can be found in *A Marianne Moore Reader* (New York, 1961, pp. 226-29).

Miss Bishop's friend and fellow poet Lloyd Frankenberg has written admiringly of "The Map" and some other poems in *Pleasure Dome* (Boston, 1949). Randall Jarrell's excellent assessment of *Poems: North & South—A Cold Spring* appears in his book *Poetry and the Age* (New York, 1959, pp. 212-14). Among the most intelligent reviews of the same book is Howard Nemerov's article in *Poetry* (December, 1955) which offers some acute observations with regard to the relationship Miss Bishop perceives to exist between nature and morality. Nemerov, however, dismisses with unnecessary condescension what he calls the "nervous and unsettled rhythms" of "A Miracle for Breakfast."

Wallace Fowlie, writing of "The Poetry of Silence" in *Commonweal* (February 15, 1957) fails to understand what I take to be Miss Bishop's principal strength as a poet—that is, her awareness of the ambiguous nature of human experience. Mr. Fowlie writes of art as if it were the single imperishable fact in ephemeral nature and of poetry as if it were a mystical religion in which a poem is drawn (in the manner of Mallarmé) "not so much from the language as from the silence of the poet." Because he wraps Miss Bishop's poems in this misty sanctity he is unable to perceive the subtlety of her insights. But Mr. Fowlie does draw attention to the way in which Miss Bishop transforms the world she describes into her world.

The British critic A. Alvarez reviewed *Poems: North & South—A Cold Spring* for the *Kenyon Review* in 1955. He is not among Miss Bishop's most enthusiastic admirers and perhaps for this reason his remarks have a justness that Mr. Fowlie's do not. He rightly suggests that she is in debt to Imagism, and he draws attention to her tone, which he distinguishes from style. Mr. Alvarez, however, misses the profundity of many of her poems because he takes them too much at face value as pieces of mere description.

By far the most perceptive criticism of Miss Bishop's work that I have seen can be found in an article entitled "Some Younger American Poets" by G. S. Fraser which appeared in the Jewish journal *Commentary* (May, 1957). Mr. Fraser, alone of all the critics I have read, realizes how dramatic and emblematic is the inclusiveness of Faustina's expression in "Faustina or Rock Roses." He comments on the straightforwardness of Miss Bishop's diction which does not eschew trite phrases when they are, as he puts it, "the *right* trite phrases" for the situations described in the poems. His remarks on Miss Bishop's extraordinary precision are backed by his intelligent understanding of what she has to say. Indeed, the entire article is worth reading carefully. It criticizes American poets of the 1950's for producing in many cases poetry which was a luxury item instead of an essential ingredient in life; it suggests that British poets of the modern era have had more to say about social and moral issues than their American contemporaries who, while producing more polished poems, have sometimes lost contact with the audience to which they should be speaking. Miss Bishop, Mr. Fraser contends, is one of the exceptions to this (he admits) overgeneralized rule. She has "an immense sense of responsibility toward a critically cooperative audience" because she herself has a sense of responsibility toward *exactly* what her poems want to say. This is the kind of recognition Miss Bishop deserves.

Notes and References

Chapter One

1. "In the Village" appeared in *The New Yorker*, XXIX (Dec. 19, 1953), 26-34 © 1953, The New Yorker Magazine, Inc. Reprinted in *Questions of Travel* (New York, 1965). Robert Lowell wrote a poem entitled "The Scream" on the same subject which appeared in *The Kenyon Review*, XXIX (Autumn, 1962), 4.

2. See *The New Yorker*, XXIX (June 27, 1953), 26-31 © 1953.

3. Emerson's essay on Nature provides an interesting contrast in attitude; while Elizabeth Bishop feels she owes much to the New England Transcendentalists, her sense of nature is hardly religious. Yet no poet of the nineteenth century felt more strongly the power of nature than she does.

4. See Helena Morley's Preface, *The Diary of 'Helena Morley'* (New York, 1957), p. xxxvi.

5. "In Prison" first apeared in *The Partisan Review*, IV (March, 1938), 4.

Chapter Two

1. Randall Jarrell has compared the poems of Elizabeth Bishop to the paintings of the French Impressionist, Edouard Vuillard. Miss Bishop is not an admirer of Wyeth's pictures and prefers Jarrell's analogy. Nevertheless, in pure, hard quality of detail, Miss Bishop's poems and Mr. Wyeth's pictures have much in common. Both are illuminated by the same, uncompromising New England light.

2. Erich Heller, *Thomas Mann, The Ironic German* (Cleveland, 1961), pp. 22-23.

3. I am fully aware of the impossibility of using this word in any philosophically satisfying sense. Since it is beyond the scope of this chapter to consider the nature of reality, the reader will have to understand the word to mean any true experience that can be publicly accepted as "real." Psychological experiences (dreams, hallucinations, fantasies) are "real" insofar as they can be mental phenomena. The concept of reality in modern literature is discussed in greater detail in Chapter V.

4. From Francis Steegmuller's translation of "Esprit Nouveau

et les Poètes" in *Apollinaire: Poet Among the Painters* (Toronto, Ambassador Books, 1964), pp. 219-20.

5. See Paul Valéry's *The Art of Poetry*, trans. Denise Folliot (New York, Vintage Books, 1961), p. 61.

6. Quoted from Giorgio di Chirico's *Autobiography* in Hugo Munsterberg, *Twentieth Century Painting* (New York, The Philosophical Library, 1951), p. 61.

7. In one of her letters Elizabeth Bishop remarks that "The Monument" was written under the influence of a set of frottages by Max Ernst called *Histoire Naturel*.

8. Arnold Hauser, *The Philosophy of Art History* (New York, 1958), p. 80.

9. *Ibid.*, p. 65.

Chapter Three

1. From Ezra Pound's "Credo" in *The Literary Essays of Ezra Pound*, ed. T. S. Eliot (Norfolk, Conn., 1952), pp. 9-10.

2. Quoted in Hugh Kenner's *The Poetry of Ezra Pound* (Norfolk, Conn., New Directions, n.d.), p. 73.

3. From Ezra Pound's "Credo," *loc. cit.*

4. See I. A. Richards, *The Philosophy of Rhetoric* (London, 1936), chapters V, VI.

5. Resonance, of course, can also refer to the musical or tonal value of words in poetry. This use of the term is an important and familiar one, but it would be confusing to introduce it here.

6. For Pound's own comments on "In a Station in the Metro" see his *Gaudier-Brzeska: A Memoir* (London, and New York, Laidlaw & Laidlaw, 1936), p. 103.

Chapter Four

1. Wallace Stevens, "The Snowman," *The Collected Poems of Wallace Stevens* (London, Faber and Faber, 1964), pp. 9-10.

2. *Ibid.*, p. 320.

3. *Ibid.*, pp. 47-48.

4. See Marianne Moore's "Virginia Britannia," *A Marianne Moore Reader* (New York, 1961), pp. 28-32.

5. Jules Laforgue, "Complainte de la Bonne Defunte," *The Poems of Jules Laforgue*, trans. Patricia Terry (Berkeley and Los Angeles, 1958), p. 24.

Chapter Five

1. E. H. Gombrich, *Art and Illusion* (London, 1962) is the best study I know of the way in which the visual properties of art relate to psychology. This book seems to me indispensable to anyone who is interested in the philosophy of art generally.

2. Wallace Stevens, "Esthetique du Mal," *op. cit.,* p. 317.

3. *Ibid.,* pp. 99-107.

4. *Ibid.,* "Six Significant Landscapes," Part VI, p. 75

5. *Ibid.,* p. 295.

6. Ludwig Wittgenstein, *Philosophical Investigations,* trans. G. E. M. Anscombe (Oxford, 1963), p. ix°.

7. *Ibid.,* p. 100°.

8. *Ibid.,* p. 145°.

9. *Ibid.,* p. 187°.

10. *Ibid.,* p. 200°.

11. Quoted from Freidrich Waismann, *Introduction to Mathematical Thinking,* trans. Theodore J. Benac (New York, 1951) p. 244.

12. See Roberto Bonola's *Non-Euclidian Geometry* (New York, 1955). The passage quoted is from Dr. Bruce Halsted's introduction to Bolyai's *The Science of Absolute Space,* p. xxviii.

13. David Bohm, *Causality and Chance in Modern Physics* (London, 1957), p. 170. See Chapter III, part iv, for as clear an explanation of the indeterminacy principle as is perhaps possible for a layman to understand. In effect, what the principle means is that the very act of observing particles interferes with their behavior: . . . "there is a reciprocal relationship between the possible precision of definition of the momentum and that of position. The more accurately the position is determined, the less accurately the momentum can be defined, and vice versa." According to Heisenberg, this means that "*every* process of measurement will be subject to . . . limitations." It is impossible ever to measure the movement of subatomic particles *absolutely.*

14. See Randall Jarrell, *Poetry and the Age* (New York, 1956), p. 45 ff.

15. Will Grohmann, *Paul Klee* (New York, n.d.), p. 99.

16. See the passage quoted from one of Elizabeth Bishop's letters on page 66.

17. See Marianne Moore, "In Distrust of Merits," *A Marianne Moore Reader* (New York, 1961), p. 43.

18. See Wallace Stevens, "Peter Quince at the Clavier," *op. cit.*, p. 89.

19. It is interesting to contrast Marianne Moore's "The Pangolin" (*A Marianne Moore Reader,* pp. 36-39) with Elizabeth Bishop's "Roosters." Miss Moore also concludes her poem with an image of the rising sun. However, the sun here is not an ambiguous symbol as it is in "Roosters" (either enemy *or* friend) but a resounding symbol of unequivocal human triumph. The pangolin is an allegorical animal in Miss Moore's poem, an emblem of man's courage, humor, kindness, grace, etc. The sun restores the pangolin's faith. These are the final lines:

> Again the sun!
> anew each day; and new and new and new,
> that comes into and steadies my soul.

Selected Bibliography

PRIMARY SOURCES

1. Books

North & South. Boston: Houghton Mifflin Co., 1946.

Poems: North & South—A Cold Spring. Boston: Houghton Mifflin Co., 1955.

The Diary of 'Helena Morley.' Translated and edited by ELIZABETH BISHOP. New York: Farrar, Straus and Cudahy, 1957.

Brazil (with the editors of *Life* for the Life World Library). New York: Time Inc., 1962.

Questions of Travel. New York: Farrar, Straus & Giroux, Inc., 1965.

2. Other Publications

"In Prison" (short story), *The Partisan Review,* IV (March, 1938).

"What the Young Man said to the Psalmist" (poem), *Poetry,* LXXIX (January, 1952), 212-14.

"Gwendolyn" (short story), XXIX (June 27, 1953), 26-31.

"Manipulation of Mirrors" (poem), *The New Republic,* CXXXV (November 19, 1956), 23-24.

"Wit" (poem), *The New Republic,* CXXXIV (February 13, 1956), 17.

SECONDARY SOURCES

BALAKIAN, ANNA. *Surrealism: The Road to the Absolute.* New York: The Noonday Press, 1959. An introduction to Surrealism written by an enthusiast.

BOHM, DAVID. *Causality and Chance in Modern Physics.* London: Routledge & Kegan Paul Ltd., 1957. A somewhat controversial book on modern physics. Of interest to this study only in so far as science *unintentionally* affects the poet's world.

BONOLA, ROBERTO. *Non-Euclidian Geometry.* New York: Dover Publications, 1955. A book of essays *not* for laymen. Interesting as an example of what concerns mathematicians.

DEUTSCH, BABETTE. *Poetry in Our Time.* New York: Doubleday & Co., 1963. See particularly pp. 269-85. The book is a readable and thorough survey of recent poetry in America and England.

COFFMAN, STANLEY K. JR. *Imagism*, Norman, Oklahoma: University of Oklahoma Press, 1951. A good introduction to the theories of the Imagists.

FRANKENBERG, LLOYD. *Pleasure Dome*. Boston: Houghton Mifflin Co., 1949. Discussed in the section on Miss Bishop's critics. A book worth reading.

FROTHINGHAM, OCTAVIUS BROOKS. *Transcendentalism in New England* New York: Harper Torchbooks, 1959. An old fashioned but excellent "classic" on the Transcendentalist movement in New England and its European origins.

GOMBRICH, ERNST H. *Art and Illusion*. London: Phaidon Press Ltd., 1962. An excellent and very original study of the psychology of art.

GRENE, MARJORIE. *Introduction to Existentialism*. Chicago, 1959. As good an introduction to this kind of philosophy as there is.

GROHMANN, WILL. *Paul Klee*. New York: Harry N. Abrams Inc., n.d. A large illustrated critical biography.

HAUSER, ARNOLD. *The Philosophy of Art History*. New York: Knopf, 1958. An excellent study of sociology and art.

HELLER, ERICH. *Thomas Mann, The Ironic German*. Cleveland: The World Publishing Company (reprinted by arrangement with Little Brown & Co.), 1961. Especially interesting discussion of early modernists.

JARRELL, RANDALL. *Poetry and the Age*. New York: Vintage Books, 1959. Essay relative to Elizabeth Bishop on pp. 212-14. The entire book is excellent, witty and perceptive.

LAFORGUE, JULES. *The Poems of Jules Laforgue*. Trans. with introduction by PATRICIA TERRY. Berkeley and Los Angeles: Univery of California Press, 1958. These translations are careful and tasteful.

MOORE, MARIANNE. *A Marianne Moore Reader*. New York: The Viking Press, 1961. Miss Moore's criticism is erratic and idiosyncratic but always worth reading. Truth gleams through illogical crevices.

POUND, EZRA. *Literary Essays*, ed. T. S. ELIOT. Norfolk, Conn.: New Directions, 1962. The standard edition of Pound's Essays.

RICHARDS, I. A. *The Philosophy of Rhetoric*. London: Oxford University Press, 1936. A little-known but very fine book by this distinguished critic.

WAISMANN, FRIEDRICH. *Introduction to Mathematical Thinking*. New York: Frederick Ungar Publishing Co., 1951. The last chapter was a source of some ideas suggested in Chapter V of this book.

WINSLOW, ANN. *Trial Balances,* New York, 1935. An Anthology. Includes a selection of poems by Elizabeth Bishop with comments by Marianne Moore.

WITTGENSTEIN, LUDWIG. *Philosophical Investigations.* Trans. G. E. M. ANSCOMBE. Oxford: Basil Blackwell, 1963. Also of interest are Wittgenstein's *Notebooks,* trans. G. H. von Wright and G. E. M. Anscombe (Oxford: Basil Blackwell, 1961). I am conscious of having used Wittgenstein's ideas in a very unphilosophical fashion. I have not of course ventured, in my book, to speak of *philosophy* at all. I was concerned only to suggest that philosophy sometimes has poetic overtones.

Index

Index

Index

MacLeish, Archibald, 47
Melville, Herman (*Moby Dick, Pierre*), 32
Metaphor, 55-56, in modern and traditional poetry, 78-79; Elizabeth Bishop's uses of, 80-94; personification and the "pathetic fallacy," 97-98 (*see also* "Tenor" *and* "Vehicle")
Mexico, 18, 43
Middleton, Christopher, 49
Millay, Edna St. Vincent, 35
Moore, Marianne, 18, 45, 46, 49, 66, 76, 87, 102, 121, 128, 134

Nature, Elizabeth Bishop's concept of, 32-33; in "Pope's Garden," 40; in "In Prison," 41; in "A Cold Spring," 89-90; as related to personification, 98-105
Nemerov, Howard, 128
Neruda, Pablo, 18, 46
Newfoundland, 42-43
New York City, 43, 47, 83
The New Yorker magazine, 18, 27, 48
Non-Euclidean geometries, 118
Nova Scotia, 25, 26, 27, 77
New England Transcendentalists, 32

The Partisan Review, 44, 46
Pascal, Blaise, 119
"Pathetic fallacy," 97
Personification, 97-105
Petrópolis, Brazil, 47
Plato, 110
Pound, Ezra, 46, 76-77, 86, 88, 120
Precision, 84-94 (*see also* Resonance, Metaphor, Images)

Reality, concepts of in twentieth century art, 58-59, 120-25; in twentieth century mathematics and science, 118; as a philosophical question, 114-16
Resonance, 84-94 (*see also* Precision, Metaphor, Images)

Richards, I. A., "tenor" and "vehicle" as terms of metaphor, 78-79
Rimbaud, Arthur, 57, 77
Rio de Janiero, 49
Robbe-Grillet, Alain, 57
Ruskin, John, *see* "Pathetic fallacy"

Schoenberg, Arnold, 57
Sidney, Sir Philip, 78
Shakespeare, William, 78
Soares, Lota de Macedo, 47
Stein, Gertrude, 57
Stevens, Wallace, 43, 49, 51, 52, 76, 98, 100, 104, 110-14, 121, 122
Surrealism, 38, 57, 58-60, 119-20
Syllabic stanzas, 45
Swift, Jonathan (*Gulliver's Travels*), 63
Symbols, in the psychology of art, 71; in Elizabeth Bishop's poems, 68-73; images as symbols, 80-84, 85

Tennyson, Alfred, 64, 85, 87
"Tenor," 78-80, 83, (*see* Richards, I. A., *and* Metaphor)

Valéry, Paul, 59
Vassar College, 25, 35, 40, 42, 45
Vassar Review, 36
"Vehicle," 78-79, 80, 83, (*see* Richards, I. A., *and* Metaphor)

Walnut Hill School, 35
"The Waste Land," poem by T. S. Eliot, 79
Washington, D.C., 18, 46
Webern, Anton von, 57, 121
Wellfleet, Cape Cod, 35
Whitman, Walt, 35, 77
Williams, William Carlos, 44, 52, 76
Winslow, Ann, 128
Wordsworth, William, 102
Worcester, Massachusetts, 25, 34
Wittgenstein, Ludwig, 57, 60; the question of the meaning of appearances, 114-17
Wyeth, Andrew, 52, 68

[143]